On Collective Goods, Voluntary Contributions, and Fundraising

Alexander von Kotzebue

On Collective Goods, Voluntary Contributions, and Fundraising

Springer Gabler

Alexander von Kotzebue
Karlsruhe, Germany

Zugl.: Dissertation, Karlsruher Institut für Technologie (KIT), 2013
Gefördert durch die Deutsche Forschungsgemeinschaft (DFG)

ISBN 978-3-658-04011-6 ISBN 978-3-658-04012-3 (eBook)
DOI 10.1007/978-3-658-04012-3

The Deutsche Nationalbibliothek lists this publication in the Deutsche Nationalbibliografie; detailed bibliographic data are available in the Internet at http://dnb.d-nb.de.

Springer Gabler

Printed on acid-free paper

Springer Gabler is a brand of Springer DE.
Springer DE is part of Springer Science+Business Media.
www.springer-gabler.de

Acknowledgements

This thesis was prepared during my time as a research assistant at the Chair of Economics and Public Finance at the FAU Erlangen-Nuremberg and at the Chair of Public Finance and Public Management at the Karlsruhe Institute of Technology (KIT). It is also the result of a research cooperation with the Centre for European Economic Research (ZEW).

First and foremost, I am deeply grateful to my supervisor Professor Dr. Berthold U. Wigger who not only supported and monitored the development of this work, but was a collaborative and sympathetic superior throughout. I also wish to thank Professor Dr. Bernd Süßmuth, who readily consented to function as second advisor, and the earlier collaboration with whom I will always remember as most pleasant and fruitful. I also owe many thanks to Professor Dr. Wolf Fichtner and Professor Dr. J. Philipp Reiß as members of the examination board.

This work was partly funded by the German Research Foundation (DFG), which thereby permitted to set up a research cooperation with the ZEW and the market research company GfK. The GfK's courtesy, and particularly Roland Adler's personal commitment provided me with an otherwise unattainable dataset, which was downright crucial for my work. I heartily thank Dr. Friedrich Heinemann and Dr. Sarah Borgloh for the cooperation and support throughout our common DFG-project, and during my research stay in Mannheim.

I am grateful to have had the opportunity to work with many wonderful colleagues in Nuremberg and Karlsruhe, especially so with Robert Dehm. The Bavarian Graduate Program in Economics (BGPE) deserves ample credit for organising excellent courses and moreover fostering networks among postgraduates in (and beyond) Bavaria.

My beloved parents encouraged and supported my work all along, and I will always be indebted to them.

Last, I most deeply thank Agnes, my dearest and closest companion, and my love.

Alexander von Kotzebue

Contents

List of Tables

List of Figures

1 Introduction

This study is concerned with the interdependency of private contributions to collective concerns, intermediate fundraising institutions, and governmental intervention.

The constituent property of a collective good is that one agent can consume it without narrowing the consumption opportunities of any other agent. In addition, it may be prohibitively costly to exclude single members of the collectivity from its consumption. So, for any rational individual, free-riding is the optimal choice.

Charitable giving, or philanthropy, is a special event of a collective good. Supporting a humanitarian cause, for instance, does not only affect the own utility, and that of the recipient, but also that of the potentially large collectivity of individuals that appreciates humanitarian aid.

Regarding the charity market, one can hence distinguish three agents: the donor, the recipient, and (a fraction of) the public. Since the emergence of collective goods is a classical justification of governmental intervention, charitable giving is naturally intermingled with governmental objectives. An obvious case in point are donations to the needy that interrelate with public poverty alleviation programmes.

This study builds on three research papers that are concerned with the literature on voluntary giving, with a theoretical model of the donor-fundraiser relation, and finally, a micro-econometric assessment of the impact of fundraising on individual charitable giving.

Private Contributions to Collective Concerns: Modelling Donor Behaviour. Chapter 2 gives account to a wide range of theoretical approaches and empirical studies on donor motivation, and the role of intermediation, i. e., of fundraising institutions.[1]

As opposed to the classic theory of public goods, empirical studies and evidence from experimental economics point towards considerable levels of private contributions dedicated to

[1] Cf., von Kotzebue and Wigger (2010).

the support of public interests. Whilst concentrating on models of donor motivation, Chapter 2 introduces a sample of theoretical approaches, groups them according to their central assumptions, and assesses their empirical relevance.

Charitable Giving and Fundraising: When Beneficiaries Bother Benefactors. Chapter 3 presents a theorical approach that elucidates the strategic interaction of fundraiser and donor, and a potential role for government.[2]

In the analysis, it is taken for granted that fundraising activities are an integral part of the process of voluntary contributions to collective matters, and that they have some impact on benefactor utility. The approach at hand is to model the potential conflict between benefactor and beneficiary with respect to the extent of fundraising activities. First, a decentral efficiency enhancing strategy is discussed, then it is demonstrated that by granting benefactors a tax privilege, governmental intervention may ease the conflict, as well.

An Empirical Investigation of Donor-Fundraiser Interaction. Chapter 4 introduces a considerably large, and to my knowledge unique, dataset. The empirical analysis intends to grasp determinants of charitable giving, with a special focus on the influence of fundraising effort.[3]

It is a stylised fact of the charity market that donations only occur upon solicitation. However, fundraising typically involves a more complex exchange of resources between beneficiary and benefactor, that most manifestly comes to sight in the ambiguous effect of fundraising on donor utility. In empirical studies that investigate this complex donor-fundraiser relation, a convincing link of individual-level data on donor motivation to nonprofit financial data has to date hardly been achieved. However, characteristics of the two extensive datasets I employ in this study permit such a merging.

---

[2] Cf., von Kotzebue and Wigger (2008).
[3] Cf., von Kotzebue and Wigger (2013).

2 Collective Goods, Voluntary Contributions, and Intermediation: A Literature Survey

"... no decentralized pricing system can serve to determine optimally [the] levels of collective consumption." Paul A. Samuelson (1954), p. 388.

The obvious discrepancy between the predictions of the standard model of private provision of public goods and empirical indications have led many economists to search for alternative explanations of the phenomenon of voluntary contributions. Whilst concentrating on models of donor motivation, the following chapter gives a non-technical survey of a sample of these approaches, and discusses their advantages and limitations.

2.1 Motivation

The standard theory of public goods neglects the possibility of meeting collective needs sufficiently through private contributions. The constituent attribute of a public or collective good is that one person can take advantage of it without cutting back the consumption opportunities of others. In addition, it may be prohibitively costly to exclude single members of society from its consumption. Taken into account the assumption of rational, and at least partly egoistic individual motives, free-riding is the individually optimal action. A free-rider will participate in the consumption of the good, yet not in its provision.

Indeed there are means of overcoming the problem by improving the organisation and coordination of the collectivity. Notably, Olson (1965) focussed on this context. Whether or not an improvement to a setting without cooperation can be achieved, does, however, crucially depend on the collectivity's size. In Olson's non-technical theoretical framework collectively rational outcomes can be expected only in environments with intensive social control, and therefore principally in small groups.

However, empirical studies and evidence from experimental economics point towards remarkable levels of private initiatives dedicated to the support or actually complete funding of public interests, even in large collectivities. For instance, charitable organisations like the Red Cross and overseas famine relief organisations, or other institutions of public interest like local sports facilities and universities are to some varying, yet undeniable extent financed by voluntary donations.[1] What is more, they often rely heavily on voluntary work. Field and laboratory experiments deliver additional strong support for the prominence of individual cooperation motives in social contexts.

The obvious discrepancy between the predictions of the standard public goods model and empirical indications have led many economists to search for alternative explanations of the phenomenon. Yet, the aim cannot be to introduce an all-embracing model of human economic behaviour. It may be strongly doubted that such a model will at all exist. And if it does, it may be expected to be exceedingly complicated. In some contexts, differences in behaviour may occur according to, e. g., religious or cultural affiliation, gender, or to the relative social position. In others, it may make a difference, whether donor and recipient belong to the same

[1] Conceptually speaking, individuals belong to many different collectivities simultaneously. Nutrition shipments are a collective good to all those who care for overseas famine relief, a team set of hockey sticks to all those who support local sports facilities.

social or geographical environment, or if the setting is completely anonymous. Therefore, most approaches choose to propose simple, and very specific structures that account for just as specific problems or observations. Younger developments will not automatically falsify older ones, but may contribute to the understanding of their range of application, their functioning and their restrictions. Nonetheless, good models should be well adaptable to a larger scope, and they should not ignore human heterogeneity.

Whilst concentrating on models of donor motivation, and only alluding to other agents' objectives, this chapter introduces a sample of those approaches, groups them according to their central assumptions, and presents their core results. The following section will be concerned with models of individual rationality, whereas the third will confront their results with those when assuming morally conscious individuals. The fourth section will scrutinise the impact of intermediary institutions, such as fundraisers, on the individual donor's utility. Section 2.5 introduces a model that embraces donor motives from all three domains. The survey closes with some concluding remarks.

2.2 Models of Individual Rationality

Positive models of private contributions to collective needs can basically be distinguished according to whether they are based on the assumption of individual rationality or on that of individual morality. Individual rationality means that the agents in question follow a well-defined objective, that they systematically use their resources and endowments to optimise (usually: maximise) their own welfare or utility. By contrast, individual morality suggests that an agent's behaviour is guided not only by self-oriented objectives, but at least to some extent by a superordinate moral notion that also takes others' concerns into account.

I will begin by describing in more detail the outcome and implications of the standard public goods approach, which can be counted among the models of individual rationality. Subsequently, I will show with which modifications more recent models try to overcome the standard model's lack of prediction power.

2.2.1 The Public Goods Model and its Empirical Shortfalls

Essentially influenced by Becker (1974), Warr (1982, 1983) and Roberts (1984), the modern version of the public goods model was cohesively restated by Bergstrom et al. (1986). According to the basic assumptions of the standard model, the individual's objective is solely influenced by her wish to consume the collective good by herself or to guarantee a certain supply. Hence, individual utility from the public good is affected only by the level of its provision. Alternative determinants such as the welfare of other members of society do not enter her calculus in any form.

In summary, when an individual decides to contribute time or money[2], she does so because she is in need of the good provided. However, the individual's gift does not only affect her own utility, but that of all other members of the collectivity – and vice versa. In large, i. e. anonymous, societies, this interdependence establishes a strong incentive to take advantage of the good's provision without bearing a suitable cost. The result generally is an inefficiently low supply of collective goods, because all individuals tend to behave in a likewise manner. This is not the only implication of the standard model, though. Further propositions are that, under quite general assumptions, neither the level of provision of the public good nor the individuals' private consumption are affected by moderate redistributions among the contributors or by "small" variations of a tax-financed governmental grant. In both cases the individuals adjust their donations such that the total supply remains unchanged.

Considering the effect of redistributions, this result is often referred to as the neutrality theorem of public goods provision. It can be summarised as follows:

Neutrality Theorem. A redistribution of income among the contributors to a public good has no effect on the total supply of the public good and on the individual consumption of the private good, as long as no individual loses more income than what she had dedicated to the supply of the good before.

Because the original bundle of private consumption and public good supply is still attainable, such a redistribution does not alter the individually optimal allocation of resources. Hence, neutrality is due to the fact that every individual reduces or raises her donation by precisely the extent to which her income has changed in consequence of the redistribution. Since the individually rational consumption plan is naturally invariant and can still be put through, the consumer will continuingly seek to fulfill it.

For large economies, even such redistributions that upset the initial resource constraints are approximately neutral, as is demonstrated in Andreoni (1988).

[2] With minor extensions to the basic model, Duncan (1999) derives the result that, in equilibrium, voluntary work and voluntary donations are perfect substitutes from the contributor's point of view.

A comparable, yet more special result can be derived when accounting for governmental initiative in terms of tax-financed provision of the collective good. The analysis of this interdependence of private and governmental supply of public goods has been motivated by Warr (1982) and Roberts (1984), and was again contiguously rephrased by Bergstrom et al. (1986). The core result of their analysis is that tax-financed contributions completely offset privately financed contributions. This proposition is often referred to as the crowding out theorem of public goods provision and can be reproduced in the following way:

Crowding Out Theorem. As long as the individual's tax burden levied to fund the public good does not exceed her original voluntary contribution, the governmental grant reduces total private provision by precisely the same extent.

The crowding out theorem is based on the same mechanism as the neutrality theorem. This is not surprising: From the donor's point of view, the government is perceived as only yet another individual ready to contribute to the collective good. So, if the government decides to take part in the provision of the public good and finances its contingent by taxing private contributors, then the latter will reduce their donations exactly by the amount of their individual tax load. In consequence, the sum of private and governmental provision is the same as the original supply resulting from solely voluntary contributions.

What is more, complete crowding out does not only pertain to lump-sum taxes, but may also follow a distortionary policy, as Bernheim (1986) shows. The only extra condition for this result is that all members of the collectivity are linked by the sequence of transfers in question. Andreoni (1988) states that even distortionary *subsidies* may be neutral, if they occur in the form of partial reductions of an individual's tax bill.[3]

However, if the redistribution of income or the taxation of individuals is such that it changes the set of contributors, i.e. that it affects former free-riders or overtaxes contributors, then both measures actually will have an effect on the total supply of the public good. In particular, a

3 In Andreoni and Bergstrom (1996), this model is restated and compared to a similar one, where subsidies actually do increase the overall provision of a collective good. If subsidies are not modelled as rebates that reduce a *universally* binding tax load, but are financed by *individually* fitted shares of total subsidy expenditures, the result is a positive relation between subsidy rate and supply level. Kirchsteiger and Puppe (1997) study the possibility to enhance a welfare-maximizing provision of public goods by means of distortionary subsidy schemes. The case where efficient supply is the unique equilibrium, is conditional on perfect information about individual characteristics.

tax-financed governmental contribution will lead to a higher level of provision, if those who do not voluntarily participate in the financing of the good are drawn on as taxpayers.[4]

Hence, it is of interest, under which circumstances and to which extent free-riding occurs in collectivities of strictly rational individuals in the first place. Whether or not single members of the society are ready to contribute to the provision of the public good, crucially depends on the size of the collectivity in question. As Andreoni (1988) demonstrates, the settings of the standard public goods model inevitably lead to the phenomenon of free-riding in large economies.

Free-rider Theorem. Consider a collectivity of n individuals, with individual wealth drawn from a continuous probability density function. Let n converge to infinity, then none but the wealthiest individual contributes a positive amount to the provision of a public good. While total provision approaches a constant positive value, the average individual donation converges to zero.

This reasoning does not rest on the presupposition of identical preferences. At the limit, though, all "remaining" contributors are of the same type.

To conclude, the standard model leads to the following propositions concerning the privately supplied level of provision of public goods and the role of governmental supply. Tax-financed governmental grants as well as tax rebates for private donations will not extend the supply of a public good, if exclusively former voluntary contributors are drawn on. Also, an exogenous redistribution of income among these individuals will have no impact on the level of supply. Involving free-riders will lead to a positive quantitative effect of governmental intervention only if the respective collectivity is small. In large economies, neutrality and crowding out approximately hold, even if non-contributors are affected.

In the standard model, there is no role for governmental intervention. From a welfare perspective, however, a case can be made for a subsidisation of charitable donations. The positive externalities imposed on the collectivity by an individual's choice to contribute may not be incorporated in her reasoning. Tax privileges can then be interpreted as Pigouvian subsidies.[5]

---

4 Bernheim (1986), by contrast, claims that under quite general circumstances even such redistributions that involve non-contributors to a good, have no impact on total supply. If more than one collective good is supplied, and there is "sufficient overlap between the sets of donors to different causes", neutrality and crowding out always take effect.

5 Blumkin and Sadka (2007) point out that, while this is true for purely altruistic motives, *taxation* of charitable contributions can be backed with the same argument in case of purely egoistic motives.

Mark that the three major results cited in this section hold true only if both the private and the public good are normal in consumption for all members of the collectivity. A rise in income entails the propensity to spend more on the collective good, and a rise in others' contributions to the good lowers the incentive to participate oneself. This requirement ensures the existence of a unique Nash equilibrium. If the collective good were not normal for each and every individual, then the effect of income redistributions could not be generally assessed.

The standard model's testable implications – (approximative) neutrality, crowding out, and free-riding – have indeed frequently been confronted with empirical data. The results can be summarised as follows:

- Exogenous redistributions do not show to be neutral.

  For examples of relevant empirical studies, see e. g. Hochman and Rogers (1973), Khanna et al. (1995), p. 268.

- Crowding out of private contributions through tax-financed governmental supply does not appear to be total.

  See e. g. Abrams and Schmitz (1978, 1984), Clotfelter (1985), Kingma (1989), Posnett and Sandler (1989), Khanna et al. (1995), Payne (1998), Eckel et al. (2005). For surveys on empirical evidence on crowding out, see Steinberg (1991), Peloza and Steel (2005) offer a meta-analysis. An interesting result is derived in a field experiment by Karlan and List (2007). They find that a matching grant enhances giving, yet that a larger rate does not outdo a lower one in terms of revenues.

- Even in large collectivities there is a notable disposition to voluntarily contribute to public concerns.

  Charitable non-profit-organisations in the US accounted for a business volume of around 600 bn US-$, or 6.2% of US-GDP, in 1999 (see Blackwell and McKee (2003)). The total of charitable contributions in the US, according to an annual survey by Giving USA, amounted to 249 bn US-$ in 2004, which exceeded 2% of GDP. Experimental evidence for a propensity to donate even in large groups and anonymous settings, and across manifold cultural environments, can be found in, e. g., Isaac et al. (1994), Ledyard (1995), Bowles and Gintis (2005), Meier (2006), and Roth et al. (1991), Henrich et al. (2001, 2004), respectively.

In reality, people obviously are not indifferent whether they contribute to the provision of a public good voluntarily or by means of transfers to the government or other individuals.[6] Besides, the absolute level of provision does not appear to be a private donor's only motive to participate in the funding of a public good. Accordingly, the assumptions of the standard model are likely to be conceptually too narrow.

2.2.2 Warm Glow

In reaction to the lack of predictive power the standard approach displays, Andreoni (1990) extends the model by a component he addresses as warm glow. Warm glow describes an abstract feeling of personal gratification arising from the act of giving itself. This sentiment is not altruistic in character, even though it might seem so from its definition. In fact, the donation is driven by the (essentially egoistic) wish to consume a purely private good, namely warm glow. The fact that an individual's donation also benefits others, is due to the non-rivalry property of collective goods, and not to her inner propulsion which remains strictly utility-maximizing.

Basically, the setting in Andreoni's approach does not differ too much from the standard model. The fundamental innovation is that the individual's contribution affects her utility not only through its impact on the overall supply, but also in a way that is completely independent of collective interests: the sheer instance of giving becomes an additional stimulus. The altruistic motive is not omitted from the individual reasoning, but now determines behaviour in conjunction with egoistic considerations. By means of this modification, Andreoni derives the following results:

- A redistribution of income among private contributors to a collective good is not neutral. In fact, the level of private provision changes due to a variation of the income distribution.
- An increase in the tax-financed governmental supply of the collective good prompts an increase in the level of total provision. Therewith, crowding out is not complete.

[6] Notwithstanding a prevalence of rejection, the outcomes of empirical tests concerning neutrality and, especially, crowding out are not completely uniform. An interesting approach to explain this disparity is provided by Borgonovi (2006): Assuming a non-linear, i. e. inverted u-shaped, influence of public support on private initiative will produce different outcomes depending on the given level of governmental intervention.

- An increase in the subsidies on private contributions to collective goods prompts an increase in the level of total provision.
- For a given level of governmental revenues, subsidies provoke a larger increase in the level of total provision than a direct governmental grant of the same extent.
- From the point of view of social welfare, subsidies are preferable to an increase of the same extent in the direct governmental grant.

Therewith the modified framework of the warm glow model leads to predictions that more easily comply with the results of empirical observations than those of the standard approach. In the equilibrium of the warm glow setting, redistributions of income will not be neutral, so there is space for an effective coexistence of private and governmental initiative. Besides, the seizable policy proposal can be derived that subsidisation of private contributions – e. g. by means of tax deductions – typically outdoes direct grants to collective goods.[7]

A paper by Ribar and Wilhelm (2002) suggests, by contrast, that a similar limit property to that producing approximative neutrality in the standard model, also strikes through to Andreoni's impure altruism approach. As long as individuals in an infinitely large collectivity do not act *purely egoistic*, their choices will completely countervail exogenous changes in the collective good's supply. A tax-financed governmental grant of one dollar, for instance, will only partly crowd out a given individual's private contribution, and therefore lead to some net increase in provision lower than one dollar. This development is anticipated by another impure altruist and again partly neutralised by her contribution decision, and so on. At the limit, crowding out is again total.

2.2.3 Other Models of Individual Rationality

The widely recognised limits of the standard model's prediction power provoked numerous economists apart from Andreoni to develop models that add an egoistic element to the calculus of a private donor, notably Margolis (1982)[8] and Steinberg (1987). Steinberg's approach also treats the individual contribution as a private good, but the donation enters the individual

7 Blumkin and Sadka (2007) point out that, while a case for subsidisation can be made for purely altruistic motives, *taxation* of charitable contributions can be backed with the same (Pigouvian) argument in case of purely egoistic motives.

8 Margolis classifies an individual's total utility from her contribution in s-utility and g-utility, i. e. in utility for "self" and "group".

calculus only once. Notwithstanding its being part of the collective good for all others, it is perceived as a separate commodity by the individual herself. Hence, for any single member of the collectivity, the public good comprises only the total of all the other members' contributions, whereas the own donation is a pure private good.

Beside the private sector, government also plays a role in Steinberg's approach. There are two levels of government, each contributing to the provision of a public good. The local government charges the individuals with a proportionate income tax, whereas the central one imposes a linear-progressive tax on the income net of local deductions and voluntary contributions. A further assumption is that the individual is indifferent whether the public good is provided by means of other persons' donations, grants on behalf of the central or those on behalf of the local government – all these types of contributions are considered perfect substitutes.

The interdependence of the own donation and that of the other members of the collectivity serves as a measure of the degree of egoism the individual is driven by. If these, too, are perfect substitutes, the individual is purely altruistically motivated. In contrast, pure egoism can be presumed when the own utility is completely independent of any other's contribution.

Mixed motives imply that an increase in the exogenous (governmental as well as private) contributions can affect the individual's choice in various ways. It may result in a higher, lower, or in an unaltered contribution. Steinberg follows that a complete crowding out of private initiative through governmental grants is, at least, largely improbable.

A further implication of the model can be stated as follows:

- Given a decrease in the central government's contribution, those of the individuals and of the local administration will indeed rise, yet not enough as to compensate for the shortfall in the central government's funding share.

Steinberg's model assigns an important role to the government: without its initiative the level of provision of a public good will be lower. This implication is not strictly clear-cut, either, but it still displays a high level of robustness.

Similar to Andreoni's (1990) model, this approach of mixed motives results in more realistic propositions concerning the neutrality of transfers between the parties involved. However, it is less general as it is focused on a specific type of government, namely a federal system.

In the context of models of individual rationality, an early contribution by Guttman (1978), labelled matching principle, shall be introduced as representative for the vast normative literature attempting to develop an efficient mechanism of public goods provision.[9] As before, the Nash-conjecture that individuals treat the others' actions altogether as given, is dismissed as counterfactual. Instead, a two-stage contribution scheme is proposed that hence allows the individuals to react to the behaviour of others. In the first stage, the players determine the rate at which they promise to match the total of contributions. In the second stage they choose their own contribution in reaction to the matching rates of the others. Hence, all matching rates are known to all agents in the second stage, and the sequential design of the procedure therewith prevents naive choices.

The individual's total contribution then consists of the flat component and the matching rate applied to the sum of the others' donations. In equilibrium, each individual chooses a subsidy rate of 1, and the following result can be derived:

- Given identical agents, the matching principle leads to a unique equilibrium, in which social welfare attains an optimum.

The matching principle thus results in a complete resolution of the free-rider problem. Strictly speaking, matching is no principle of individual rationality, though. It is a mechanism that members of a collectivity can agree on against the background of their mutual welfare. However, it again relies on very strong assumptions, namely those of perfect information and identical preferences.

2.3 Models of Individual Morality

The free-rider problem has not only been analysed according to the concept of the strictly rational homo oeconomicus, it has also frequently been scrutinised against the background of other codes of conduct. That part of the related literature coined "Kantian" will be dealt with in the next section. Alongside, this chapter will be concerned with other concepts of modeling individual contributions to public goods on the basis of individual morality.

9 This normative branch of literature on voluntary contribution games is known under the name of Mechanism Design Literature. Among its most notable contributions are those by Clarke (1971) and Groves (1973) (which, based on Vickrey (1961), founded the group of so-called Vickrey-Clarke-Groves-mechanisms), Bliss and Nalebuff (1984), Bagnoli and Lipman (1989).

2.3.1 The Kantian Approach

Kant's (1785, 1907) Categorical Imperative is frequently interpreted as an individual's obligation to solely choose an action she would want everyone else to choose, too.

Categorical Imperative. "Act only on that maxim through which you can at the same time will that it should become a universal law."[10]

Effectively, such a notion of human behaviour may influence the outcome of voluntary contribution games in that it expands the range of possible levels of provision towards an efficient supply of public goods, as Bilodeau and Gravel (2004) show. The authors generalise the basic work of Laffont (1975), which is sensitive to the restrictive assumption of identical preferences and resources.

The analysis is based on the standard voluntary contribution model described by Bergstrom et al. (1986), among others. The player's strategy space is determined by her income, i. e. her individual range of possible resource allocations. In addition, private goods (such as nutrition) are assumed to be essential, whereas public goods are not. Hence, the setting is quite familiar to those presuming individual rationality. So far, the players act in basically the same environment.

The significant difference is embodied by the principles underlying the individual's choice of conduct. She does not act according to the logic of strict utility maximisation, but rather obeys the application of the Kantian norm. Also, the welfare of others does not enter the individual's calculus as in the altruistic model, where it essentially becomes a public good liable to the typical free-riding problems. Here, the preference – or even: the innate obligation – to participate arises from a cooperation motive. It seems plainly unfair not to behave in the way one expects others to do. So, individuals feel utterly indebted to act their part in satisfying collective requirements.

On the basis of these assumptions, Bilodeau and Gravel prove the existence of an equilibrium that leads to the following outcome:

- Individuals that unanimously act according to the Kantian maxim voluntarily provide the efficient level of supply of a public good.

[10] Kant (1907), p. 88.

Hence, the free-rider problem can be overcome if all individuals comply with the interpretation of the categorical imperative described above.[11]

The Kantian norm does, of course, display elements of rational choice, especially when it comes to assessing the possibility of a generalisation of other-regarding behaviour, but it will always rely on an intrinsic prosocial motivation. Anticipating that everybody else followed the Kantian rule would again give a purely rational individual an incentive to freeride. Here, however, cooperation is unconditional on the behaviour of others.

2.3.2 Other Notions of Individual Morality

Beside the Kantian approach, other notions presupposing individual morality have been developed in order to surmount the standard model's strictly inefficient outcome.

Notably, Sugden (1984) offers an approach of social exchange, whilst disclaiming as arbitrary and counterfactual the simple Nash-assumption that all agents individually act in best response to the given conduct of all other agents. Instead of treating the actions of others as given, in Sugden's approach the individuals account for the fact that their own behaviour influences that of all others – and vice versa.

Just as in the "Kantian" models, Sugden thus supposes that the members of a collectivity are led by a notion of cooperation that lets them include mutual concerns into their consideration. Yet beyond that, he criticises the application of Kantianism outlined above, because individuals agree to obey their moral obligation, irrespective of whether the others act in the same way, or not. This "principle of unconditional commitment"[12] appears to him just as unfair as unconditional free-riding, and therefore as irrelevant in practice.

Sugden presumes that every player establishes claims on what would be a universally appropriate contribution to the collective good, i. e. what she would best want every single member of the collectivity to dedicate (in the following: individually best-preferred contribution). Then, individual conduct can be appointed practically moral where it predicates on reciprocity. This norm of mutual cooperation is specified as follows:

11 The authors label their application of Kant's concept "universalisation". It has to be noted, though, that e. g. Wolfelsperger (1999) criticises the "Kantian economics" as philosophically banal. Besides, he denies the possibility of deriving a solution for the prisoner's dilemma from "authentic Kantianism" (Wolfelsperger (1999), p. 898). In fact, Kant's objective is not to create a norm of, but to deliver a positive theory for human conduct. It claims that individuals in practice incur a self-obligation to ensure the collectively rational outcome.

12 Sugden (1984), p. 774.

Reciprocity. Given that all other individuals contribute an amount g not lower than her best-preferred contribution, the individual is bound to dedicate at least g to the funding of the collective good.

As long as everybody else participates in an appropriate manner from the point of view of an individual, she will reciprocate this behaviour.[13]

The equilibrium is defined as the set of the smallest individual donations to the collective good that comply with this principle of reciprocity. In particular, equilibria will exist where the following circumstances are given:

- Each and every individual contribution to a collective good is not lower than the payment the individual would make, were she the only contributor, and not higher than her best-preferred contribution.
- Apart from the boundary case that the individually best-preferred contribution is zero, there will always exist multiple equilibria.
- Solely the specific equilibrium that consists of identical individually best-preferred contributions is optimal from the point of view of social welfare. Any other equilibrium results in an inefficiently low level of provision of the collective good.

Thus, the principle of reciprocity will only lead to a congruence of individually and collectively rational behaviour, and therewith to an efficient outcome, when accompanied by very restrictive assumptions. However, free-riding can indeed be confined, so that the phenomenon of voluntary (partial) funding of public concerns effectively can be explained by the adherence to such a behavioural norm.[14]

A notable approach in the same line is Young's (1989) fair-share model, that calls for the individuals to contribute an equal relative share of their income. The outcome is similar, too: the incentive to take advantage of the others' efforts can be limited, therewith allowing clearly higher levels of provision than predicted by the standard model.

[13] Empirical indications for such a logic of action can be found in, e. g., Fong (2001). A field experiment conducted by Frey and Meier (2004) also supports a notion of "conditional cooperation".

[14] Reciprocity as an important determinant of behaviour in voluntary contribution games is subject to more recent analysis, too - with a theoretical focus (cf. Rabin (1993)) as well as, even more prominent, in experimental economics. This large field of research is beyond the scope of this survey, yet some propositions are Fehr and Schmidt (1999), Bolton and Ockenfels (2000), Falk and Fischbacher (2006).

Chan et al. (1997) present an experiment that delivers empirical indications of a comparable norm of conduct. Their so-called equity model comes to an end that also dismisses the free-rider proposition of the altruistic setting:

- Referring to the predictions of the standard public goods model, poorer individuals contribute more, and richer individuals contribute less to the funding of the collective good.

In fact, the individual contribution converges to a constant value, so that an average donation of Zero becomes an extremely particular case.

The idea of accounting for relative levels of income (or utility) can be traced in later models of inequality aversion, where altruistic behaviour as well as non-cooperation, or even punishment, result from an individual's position in the collectivity's income distribution.[15]

To a certain extent, the above-mentioned models all depend on the complete observability of the collectivity's donation distribution. In large economies, this is quite unlikely. A model by Holländer (1990) concentrates on this aspect. It explores the individual motivation to contribute to a collective good despite the negligible impact of the donation on the good's overall level of provision. Holländer demonstrates that, also in large collectivities, a higher level of welfare can be reached if individuals are emotionally sensitive to what he calls "social approval". The model does not presuppose a clear-cut rule of conduct from the outset, but shows that the inclination towards "social approval" will lead to one such.

Members of a collectivity are assumed to care about the other members' sentiments toward them in absolute as well as relative terms. Notwithstanding the negligibly small contribution of a donor's gift to social well-being, it is subject to an approving sentiment. This is, because individuals are held to "consider the hypothetical advantage"[16] they would encounter if everybody displayed a similar comportment. Therefore, the degree of participation in the supply of a collective good, which delivers no noteworthy incentive to cooperate in large groups itself, is positively correlated with an emotional "good" provided by the fellow individuals.

Since all subjects are assumed to have the same preferences for approval, and governmental coercion rules out the possibility to gain any such award, the following result holds:

- If preferences for social approval exist, ceteris paribus, the resulting equilibrium is superior in terms of collective welfare to that enforced by government.

[15] Notions of inequality aversion can be found in, e. g., Fehr and Schmidt (1999, 2003), Bolton and Ockenfels (2000), Charness and Rabin (2002).

[16] Holländer (1990), p. 1161.

Besides, the model setting brings about the evolution of a social norm oriented at the average donation. Divergence from this guideline is responded to in either an approving or a disapproving way, depending on the direction of the deviation. So, what is presupposed by models such as that by Chan et al. (1997), or shown in experiments on inequality aversion, automatically emerges from the general setting in Holländer (1990). In consequence, individuals may agree to contribute a positive amount toward the provision of a collective good, even though their contribution remains virtually unsubstantial for the overall level of supply.

Not only the presence, but also the evolution and the diversity of other-regarding preferences in different social environments are subject to a rapidly growing literature in the field of experimental economics, and increasingly influenced by approaches from social psychology and biology. Cooperation, when deviating from utility-maximizing actions, is shown to be conditional on the likelihood that others will reciprocate (on the other hand, non-cooperation may be punished, even when it is costly to an individual).[17]

Notions of fairness and reciprocity appear to be decisive in shaping social standards, yet their materialisation differs largely across cultural environments. The impact of cultural background on the design of other-regarding norms is emphasised by, e. g., Roth et al. (1991), Henrich et al. (2001, 2004) and Henrich (2004), where the varying outcomes of the experiments seem to reflect diversities in the test subject's everyday life. The results obtained in a vast number of experiments suggest that many stylised facts of individual giving behaviour have not been captured by economic theory to date.

2.4 The Role of Intermediation

The models discussed so far widely function within the framework of a one-shot voluntary contribution game, i. e. the individuals simultaneously contribute to the provision of the collective good, which then is supplied in perfect equivalence to the value of the total fund. Accordingly, no transaction costs are assumed to exist that may reduce the amount supplied in any sense whatsoever.

In reality, though, we observe charitable organisations and fundraising institutions that generate costs when soliciting and administering private donations. So, an agent is obviously in-

[17] See, e. g., Fehr and Schmidt (1999), Fehr and Gächter (2000), Field (2001), Fehr and Fischbacher (2002), Hammerstein (2003), Bowles and Gintis (2005), Gintis et al. (2005), and Meier (2006).

terposed in the provision mechanism of some collective goods, whose presence and demeanor cannot be accounted for by the previously quoted approaches. In effect, part of the donation is transmitted to an agent who, seemingly, does not create a surplus value: she simply conveys the funds to their destination, an exercise the donor could be expected to just as well perform herself.

However, if the costs and frictions caused by these intermediate parties actually were dispensable, they should disappear in the course of the competition for donations. This development cannot be observed in reality.[18] Consequentially, the activities of such costly institutions should contain some sort of value in order to justify their presence.

Most manifest is an informational function of intermediation. A potential donor is not automatically aware of the option to take part in the funding of a certain cause. Besides, the quality of the respective good is not always easy to observe. For that reason, charitable organisations generally distribute information on their field of activity and the intended attribution of the gifts.

Beyond the mere informational function, fundraising is assumed to feature a stimulus in the provision mechanism. It may turn an initially subliminal wish to contribute into an explicit donation. A stylised fact of charity is that individuals may only contribute when directly confronted with the well-specified request to participate in a particular funding process.

Another important quality of intermediation is to accord traits of a private good to the mechanism of supply of a fundamentally public good, and so to erode the incentive to free-ride. A direct, straightforward example from fundraising is the raffle strategy.[19] Participants in such a lottery contribute to a collective cause, whilst accounting for the probability to win a certain prize.

More generally, intermediation may add a private dimension to the contribution through a visible sign of approval (that may increase with its size). Philanthropic gifts are often suspected of merely concealing egoistic interests. There is a tradition in social science, too, that supports this view.[20] Considering such a taste for reputation, an individual's utility is affected in excess of the good's mere supply, and the donation itself is in a way set apart from the body of collective contributions. An intermediate institution will best serve its cause if it re-

[18] In 1995, fundraising institutions in the US were hired by about 115,000 charitable organisations, accounting for a revenue of roughly 2 bn US-$. Cf. Money Magazine Online, cited in Andreoni (2006a).

[19] See, e. g., Morgan (2000), Morgan and Sefton (2000), Duncan (2002).

[20] See, e. g., contributions as early as Mandeville (1724).

sponds to suchlike motivated donations by offering instruments that enhance the donor's social recognition.

Some inferences on donor utility may also be drawn from the behaviour an intermediary typically displays. Models that analyse fundraising methods often propose a sequential procedure, or emphasise the role of large initial gifts.[21] This implies, that donors are interested in the progress of the funding, i. e. in its probability to succeed, when the good needs to meet a certain threshold. Andreoni (1998) studies the strategic implications of capital versus continuous campaigns before the same background. Further notable approaches modeling the donor-intermediary relation mainly from the intermediary's point of view, can be found in papers by Romano and Yildirim (2001), and Bac and Bag (2003), for instance.

In essence, a distinct classification in models of donor behaviour and of intermediary behaviour cannot be made. Naturally, where optimal fundraising strategies are analysed, they always predicate on assumptions referring to donor preferences[22].

The following sections will provide an introduction to the role of intermediate institutions on the basis of selected models of the philanthropy market. I am well aware of the fact that intermediaries naturally are exposed to specific incentive structures themselves, and therewith may display a behaviour that deviates from that taken for granted here. However, this field of research is beyond the scope of this survey. I will concentrate on the implications especially for *donor* utility.

2.4.1 Charitable Gifts as a Signal of Status

The model proposed by Glazer and Konrad (1996) accounts for the observation that, in many forms of appearance, donations are generally not made anonymously (although, incidentally, tax deductions are usually not conditional on anonymity).

The authors describe a society, where an individual's voluntary contribution to a collective good serves as a signal of wealth. An individual might wish to signal her wealth because it is seen as the fruit of extraordinary intellectual abilities or outstanding character trades. But instead of conveying the signal herself, an individual relies on an independent institution in order to add the necessary credibility to the announcement of her donation.

21 See Vesterlund (2003), and List and Lucking-Reiley (2002), Andreoni (2006), respectively.

22 The Harbaugh (1998a) prestige approach, for instance, proposes an innovative dimension in donor utility, and then derives optimal publication strategies for intermediary institutions based thereon; cf. section 2.4.2.

Compared to other proxies of wealth, such as excessive private consumption, a philanthropic gift is a powerful signal, because its publication may offer a better perceptibility. Another advantage is the generally higher social acknowledgement of charitable initiative.

According to this approach, the reason for the failure of the standard and of the warm glow model is the anonymity of the donor. Yet, the argument here is not that publication enhances social control. In large economies the sanctioning of inadequate contributions would still be prohibitively difficult. Instead, Glazer and Konrad conjecture a positive incentive to participate in the funding of a public good, namely the quest for social status. Besides, none of the previously presented models delivers a direct explanation for the frequent observation that voluntary contributions, as far as published in donor categories, are significantly overproportioned at the lower categorial boundary.[23] Obviously, individuals do not always participate for reasons of altruism, or to sense a warm glow of giving, but in order to achieve recognition in their social environment.

Glazer and Konrad model status as the individual net wealth signaled to the other members of the collectivity. The individual determines her optimal contribution on the basis of her resources. The others observe her choice and deduct rational expectations with respect to the donor's wealth.

The specification of the status model results in the following implications:

- Crowding out is not complete as long as the government finances its grant by means of lump-sum taxes.
- Redistributions are not neutral. In particular, equational redistributions raise the level of provision of the public good.
- Due to a proportional governmental subsidy of private donations that is financed by a reduction of the government's direct grant, the level of overall provision rises.

The model delivers quite natural implications such as the negation of the neutrality theorem and the preferability of tax deductions for contributors over direct grants. What is more, it offers a possible concretion for the process that might create the so far quite diffuse sense of a warm glow. Namely, what adds private utility to an individual's contribution here is the

[23] The publication of the donors' names in categories such as "Distinctive Member" or plainly "Friendly Supporter" restricts the information from the exact amount to a broad range of monetary contributions. For an empirical analysis of the resulting behaviour, see Harbaugh (1998b).

opportunity to have an intermediary institution publish her gift, and therewith to gain social acknowledgement. So, in addition to a possible informational function, charitable organisations adopt the role of a signal transmitter.

2.4.2 Prestige as a Source of Extrinsic Motivation

Harbaugh's (1998a) prestige model is based on the same observation that inspired the status model: the strikingly high percentage of contributions exactly at or just above the lower boundaries of the respective donor categories. The specification of this model constitutes an expansion to Glazer and Konrad's setting, though: Harbaugh integrates the incentives warm glow and prestige, whereby interpreting the first as a purely intrinsic, and the latter as an extrinsic source of motivation. This specification provides a number of interesting insights into the interdependence of donors and intermediaries. Particularly, the ambition for prestige establishes a scope for an intermediary to influence the donor's choice of resource allocation.

Just as in the status model, the altruism motive is completely omitted from the individual utility function. The contribution is in fact seen as a pure private good affecting the donor's calculus solely by creating prestige due to its publication and by means of an immanent experience of well-being sensed when giving.

Besides publishing a contributor's name, an intermediary might announce the exact amount issued, or the donor category. She might also make no announcement at all. Harbaugh examines which publication scheme is most desirable from the donor's point of view. Incidentally, the preferences of donor and intermediary widely coincide: an opportunity for substantial utility gains will entail a correspondingly large individual contribution, and therewith simultaneously benefit a revenue maximizing intermediary.[24]

A comparison of the three publication schemes concerning the effect on total gift revenues yields the following implications:

- Publication of the exact contribution results in a higher total revenue than making no announcement.

[24] Notwithstanding the acceptance of revenue-maximisation as the predominant motive, the intermediary's primary objective is subject to some discussion. A study by Khanna et al. (1995) suggests that, depending on their field of work, some charities appear to maximise either net or gross revenues. Others cannot be distinctly linked to any of these objectives.

- Publication within donor categories may lead to a higher, unchanged, or lower total revenue than an exact announcement.

The latter result prompts Harbaugh's further analysis of an optimal publication scheme. Given that an intermediary knows the distribution of donor types, yet not the type of a particular donor, a revenue maximizing publication scheme should satisfy the following requirements:

- Optimal publication schemes exhibit donor categories at the upper and lower margins of the gift distribution.
- Optimal publication schemes announce the exact height of medium contributions.
- Optimal publication schemes exhibit a limited number of donor categories.

Besides delivering implications for an effective reward of philanthropic initiative, the model is capable of describing the characteristics of typical organisational forms of charitable institutions.[25] Notably, intermediaries with an over-regional or international scope will presumably drive campaigns for small gifts from very many donors, because their addressees are most unlikely to interact, and therefore cannot be rewarded much prestige. Hence, only warm glow is applicable as a private motivation to give to this type of charitable organisation.

By contrast, local organisations or such operating in a network are prone to solicit larger gifts from a relatively small number of donors, which tend to be associated in some manner. Accordingly, these intermediaries display a certain amount of monopolistic power, as they are able to offer a degree of prestige that generally is inaccessible through other organisations. Alumni of an elite university, for instance, can achieve far more prestige by having their donation published in a medium addressing the graduates of precisely this university than of any other one, notwithstanding its possibly being even more elitist. The reason is quite simple: the prestigious donation can only be linked to their person by individuals who "know" them sufficiently well.

In addition, Harbaugh's approach is convenient to explain the pooling of charitable organisations. Such consolidated institutions, e. g. the "United Way", launch few, yet extensive campaigns, and divide the revenue among the charities they represent. Often, the individual

[25] Further research on the scope of charitable organisations, especially on the role of central charities in the provision of local versus global collective goods is scrutinised in, e. g., Konrad (1998), Blackwell and McKee (2003). Rose-Ackerman (1982), and Bilodeau and Slivinski (1997), among others, deliver implications on how market structure and competition may form an intermediary's specific behaviour.

organisation is small and generates only little prestige. The economies of scale linked to the expenses of solicitation, as well as the possibility to convey more prestige to the donors via local cooperations, may well lead to a higher net revenue.

2.4.3 Impact Philanthropy

Duncan (2004) addresses an individual that gains personal satisfaction from effectively and distinctly influencing the supply of a collectively beneficial good as an impact philanthropist.

Just as the public goods model, Duncan's approach implies an interdependency of individual contributions. Yet, the reaction to any other's donation runs exactly counter to that induced by the standard model. Instead of providing utility by offering the opportunity to free-ride, the initiative of other members of the collectivity spins off negative externalities. The impact philanthropist's gift produces less effect, and the given financial endowment of the good scales it down to a side note.

Impact philanthropy embeds the standard model as well as warm glow as marginal cases. The central innovation of the approach is, as noted above, that the given supply of the collective good depreciatively enters the individual's utility function, because in consequence the donation's impact on public benefit degrades.

The impact philanthropy model fulfills the empirically founded exigence that governmental grants do not neutralise private donations:

- Under quite weak assumptions, exact crowding out is impossible. By contrast, crowding in may be supported.

Another interesting result is related to the distribution of private funds on multiple collective concerns:

- The impact philanthropist will, ceteris paribus, choose that allocation that spreads her gift more unevenly among different collective goods.

This result leads to a conflict of interests between the charity and the donor. For illustration, Duncan uses the example of a child relief organisation that seeks to conduct the gifts freely, and to purposefully allocate the resources among the children.[26] By contrast, the impact philanthropist will always prefer a conditional donation, particularly restricting the number of

[26] For example, by adhering to the highest marginal impact of the single dollar, and not to that of the total gift.

beneficiaries. That is because he chooses to distinctly support one particular child rather than to sparsely aid a number of (anonymous) children. So, despite their probable disadvantageousness for the addressees, such contracts, e. g. a sponsorship for a needy child, are quite commonly concluded. The reason for the intermediaries' giving in to the claim for comparable arrangements supposedly lies in the charitable organisations' competition for donors.

2.5 A Compound Approach

Bénabou and Tirole (2007) present a model of individual behaviour in collectivities that, in a manner of speaking, encompasses the approaches presented in the sections on individual rationality and morality, and on intermediation. The authors identify three driving forces of "prosocial behavior": individual conduct is guided by an intrinsic feeling of obligation, by extrinsic incentives, and by a taste for reputation in a collectivity. The interaction between these stimuli may, however, slightly differ from the way it has been shaped in the models presented above.

Agents are intrinsically motivated when they feel liable to follow (moral) norms that either emerge endogenously from social interaction, or are due to the desire for self-contentment.[27]

Extrinsic motives refer to rewards, such as prizes in charitable raffles, rebates, or so-called fringe benefits[28]. They may, on the other hand, include penalties for deviation from some social norm. Following an observation by Titmuss (1970), the model allows for a substitutive relation between intrinsic and extrinsic motivations to contribute to a collective cause. Titmuss states that moral objectives to donate blood may be crowded out by monetary rewards, because unselfish behaviour is given a price and therewith deprived of its impact on (self-) acknowledgement.[29] So, in Bénabou and Tirole's approach, the overall effect of incentives on charitable giving is not necessarily unambiguous.

As a third force that shapes individual intrasocial conduct, the disposition towards reputation drives an agent's willingness to participate in a collective matter. By means of gift publications, for instance, the donor may signal traits such as wealth, generosity, or a sense of acquittal. But again, the signal may also have a counter-effective impact, because boasting is

27 Concerning the desire to live up to a specific self-image, see also Brekke et al. (2003).

28 Think of, e. g., preferential admittance to dress rehearsals at the opera.

29 Mellström and Johannesson (2005), among others, find evidence for such a crowding out effect in blood donation.

not acknowledged even when it is related to apparently non-selfish causes. An intense signal may, in the eyes of the others, bring to the fore the egoistic dimension of the donor's reasoning.

As in Holländer (1990), the model does not presuppose any rules of conduct, but allows for heterogeneity of individual tastes for, e. g., altruism, and describes the emergence of multiple norms of intrasocial behaviour. Individuals draw conclusions from observed behaviour, and form a pattern of interdependencies between agents' actions. The substitutability or complementarity of individuals' choices is then determined by whether conformity or deviation from "mainstream" attitudes is appreciated.

A subset of the results Bénabou and Tirole derive from their framework is the following:

- Rewards and penalties are counterproductive for a wide range of values.
- Nevertheless, agents will generally not reject rewards.
- The optimal incentive rate does not fully compensate for the donation's public good externalities.
- Competition among intermediaries will, ceteris paribus, increase rewards for donors, and therewith diminish social welfare, compared to the monopoly case.

The model reflects the complex structure of individual contribution decisions, which are driven by a medley of objectives such as altruism, status orientation, self-conception, social norms, incentive structures, and notions towards "mainstream" behaviour. These underlying structures again differ across individuals, and the driving force of the model then is the interpretation and valuation of an individual's emitted signals by the other members of the collectivity.

2.6 Concluding Remarks

The standard public goods model has shown to possess noteworthy weaknesses in prediction power. Restricting the character of a donation to merely that of a component of a collective good obviously cannot explain the prevalent level of private funding of collective concerns. An expansion of the underlying individual motivation to moral aspects or to purely private incentives such as status, prestige, or warm glow, admits a better understanding of the empirically observable behaviour a private donor typically displays. Various theoretical approaches discussed above are in line with that.

There are numerous other studies related to the investigation of the so-called voluntary sector's characteristic properties. Needless to say that this survey can only offer a sample of the quite substantial and still incessantly growing literature. While I concentrate on the individual motives of donors alone, the strategic interactions among donors as well as between donors and fundraisers receive acute attention in present research. Some core aspects of such relations, such as the role of intermediaries, were referred to above, yet again mainly within the scope of utility effects for donors. It was outlined that fundraisers should principally announce the source and height of the donation – in categories, as the case may be, yet by all means in a prestige-enhancing manner. In general, the possible trade-off between personal and collective requisitions should be adequately addressed through the arrangement of the provision process.

Various branches of research within the wide brackets of private contributions to public concerns were not explicitly addressed in this survey, yet still are of great interest. There is, as outlined before, a vast literature on mechanisms to overcome free-riding.[30] Another large field of research is concerned with experiments that study donor behaviour in a laboratory environment.[31]

Of course, an in-depth understanding of donor behaviour also has an undeniable impact on the role of government. The degree of substitutability between a donor's and the government's contribution affects the design of subsidisation schemes, or the question of optimal taxation of contributors.[32] Another issue is the measurement of social welfare, when purely private, often intangible, utility from charitable contributions is to be assessed. A discussion of whether warm glow, for instance, should be incorporated in a social planner's objective function is provided by Diamond (2006); a related discussion can be found in Bénabou and Tirole (2006).

---

30 Examples are, besides those already mentioned, Admati and Perry (1991), Varian (1994), and Marx and Matthews (2000).

31 A survey is provided, for instance, by Ledyard (1995), and Meier (2006).

32 See, e. g., Kaplow (1995), and Diamond (2006), respectively. Important empirical studies of the interdependence of governmental initiative and private donations are presented by Randolph (1995), and Auten et al. (2002).

3 A Theoretical Approach to Strategic Donor-Fundraiser Interaction

"An iron law of fundraising is that people tend not to give unless they are asked." James Andreoni (2006a, p. 1257).

Many institutions of collective interest partly or even totally depend on philanthropic gifts. Yet, such private donations usually do not occur if not distinctly solicited; an intermediate process becomes necessary, with the objective to attract potential benefactors. So, most of these entities engage in costly fundraising activities. My approach is to model the common fundraising process, and the conflict that arises between beneficiary and benefactor when the beneficiary implements more fundraising than the benefactor would deliberately choose. The resulting allocation proves inefficient. I present an efficiency-enhancing strategy, where the benefactor limits excessive fundraising through initial bounteousness. A more favourable allocation can also be achieved by a tax privilege of donations.

3.1 Motivation

Many instances partly or even totally depend on philanthropic gifts. Institutions such as a theatre, though drawing income from ticket sales, often enough hinge on supplementary governmental grants – and private donations. In pedestrian zones, one will quite frequently encounter beggars or animal rights groups that also strive towards private benevolence. The maintenance of performance operations in a theatre, or the support of needy persons are both typical examples of causes a philanthropist might wish to support. And effectively, a significant amount of voluntary contributions to suchlike purposes can be observed empirically.

Yet, private donations usually do not occur if not distinctly solicited. Accordingly, a further joint attribute of the above-mentioned examples is that fundraising activities of some sort are exercised. In response, the addressees are prompted to donate, either to satisfy a taste for giving, or because they feel coerced to do so. A theatre might offer preferential access to dress rehearsals or opening nights to its most generous benefactors, and an animal rights organisation might approach passers-by with illustrated leaflets on animal mistreatment. Quite obviously, in these cases a need for donations is not satisfied on emergence. Instead, fundraising as an intermediate device becomes necessary, with the objective to attract potential benefactors. The phenomenon that donations only occur upon solicitation is known as the "power of the ask".[1] However, fundraising generally goes beyond simply asking for gifts. Typically, it involves a more complex exchange of resources between beneficiary and benefactor, especially concerning the benefactor's utility from the provision process.

There is a growing literature that attempts to explain potential benefits for the benefactor that evolve from fundraising activities, and that is partly outlined in Chapter 2. Either fundraising simply constitutes an indispensable part of the provision process, or it brings about utility beyond altruistic concerns. The former argument is adapted in models that emphasise fixed costs and transaction costs, as in Andreoni (1998), Andreoni and Payne (2003), Vesterlund (2003), Bag and Roy (2008), and Shang and Croson (2009). Fundraising may fulfil, for instance, the function to lower the cost of information or to guarantee some threshold supply of a collective good in the presence of non-convexities.

The latter argument is reflected in the analysis of mechanisms employed by charitable institutions in order to enhance private giving. Raffle models, as presented by Morgan (2000),

[1] Andreoni (2006a, p. 1257).

Morgan and Sefton (2000), and Duncan (2002), demonstrate the effect of linking donations to the opportunity of winning a lottery prize. Other approaches, as in Glazer and Konrad (1996), Harbaugh (1998a,b), Romano and Yildirim (2001), and Bac and Bag (2003), emphasise the role of publishing the benefactor's name in conjunction with the amount given. Thus, fundraisers choose strategies that add a private dimension to the causes supported by the gift – either explicitly through a raffle, or more subtly, through gift announcements.

In the following analysis, it is taken for granted that fundraising activities are an integral part of the process of voluntary contributions to collective matters, and that they have an impact on benefactor utility. The approach at hand is to model the potential conflict between benefactor and beneficiary with respect to the *extent* of fundraising activities. Initially, I examine the case where fundraising brings about a positive marginal effect on benefactor utility, as in the theatre example. Then, I model the case where fundraising is perceived as annoying or perturbing, as in the example with illustrations of mistreated animals.

In any case, the beneficiary is assumed to prefer a strictly *higher* level of fundraising than the benefactor would deliberately choose. This presupposition is essential for the results, and rests on the argument that the beneficiary can literally compel larger gifts by offering more fundraising. She strategically exploits the strictly positive marginal effect of fundraising on giving, which results from the benefactor's feeling of innate obligation or coercion. I show that in this – so to speak natural – setting, where the beneficiary determines the outcome by her choice of fundraising, the conflict between the beneficiary and the benefactor concerning the level of fundraising results in an inefficient equilibrium.

Subsequently, two alternative strategies to remedy this inefficiency are presented. First, a decentral efficiency enhancing strategy is discussed, where the benefactor commits herself to what I call strategic bounteousness. The basic line of thought is that benefactors should limit excessive fundraising by offering a donation that is acceptable for the beneficiary in accordance with less fundraising. Where this strategy is not prevented by the institutional environment, it will enforce an efficient allocation. Then I demonstrate that governmental intervention, too, may ease the conflict. By granting benefactors a tax privilege, the price of the donation is lowered. In the resulting equilibrium, the efficiency gains mainly accrue to the beneficiary. By contrast, strategic bounteousness allows the benefactor to incorporate these gains.

The remainder of the chapter is organised as follows. Section 3.2 introduces the model and, as a benchmark, characterises the equilibrium allocation of the fundraising game. Section 3.3 establishes the notion of strategic bounteousness. Section 3.4 discusses some modifications, namely annoying fundraising and non-altruistic giving. Section 3.5 considers the effects of a tax privilege on donations, before Section 3.6 briefly concludes.

3.2 The Model

I propose a simple model, in which I intend to capture what will be referred to as the natural fundraising process. Benefactors do not make gifts without having encountered some form of fundraising. In this context, I refer to fundraising in a rather broad sense: any activity carried out by the potential recipient in order to attract, administer, or award donations, is subsumed under the term of fundraising effort. One can imagine a wide range of such activities, reaching from undirected mailings over the arrangement of a formal diner to the renaming of a university department. I think of fundraising effort as a cardinal measure, e.g., opportunity costs or Euros spent.

Consider a beneficiary approaching a representative benefactor.[2] The beneficiary dedicates some effort to fundraising, and the benefactor responds by choosing a certain donation. The beneficiary is assumed to draw utility b from the donation d net of her fundraising effort f,

$$b = d - f. \tag{3.1}$$

So, the beneficiary's utility is merely driven by the resources she can spend on the purpose she advocates. In other words, her objective is the maximisation of net revenues.

The benefactor is endowed with disposable income or wealth m, which she may choose to allocate among private consumption c, and a donation d to the beneficiary. The benefactor's utility B is an additively separable function of private consumption, and the allocation resulting

2 Note that competition among beneficiaries is excluded, and thus a certain extent of monopolistic power is ascribed to them.

from the beneficiary's net resources[3] and the corresponding level of fundraising the beneficiary offers,

$$B = u(c) + v(b, f), \tag{3.2}$$

where $m = c + d$ and $c, d \geq 0$. The functions u and v measure the utility the benefactor derives from private consumption and benevolence, respectively. With regard to the latter, there is an altruistic as well as an egoistic dimension to the benefactor's utility. The net donation is a collective good in that it is of mutual interest. Supporting a neighborhood project, for instance, will aid the recipients, and the donor will appreciate that problems in her surroundings become less. Yet, the benefactor is not only interested in the beneficiary's net revenue, but she also strictly benefits from a marginal rise in fundraising. This is purely private utility. One might think of Christmas cards from donees, of prestige-enhancing incidents such as the publication of donations, or of fringe benefits like an invitation to dress rehearsals.

In what follows, I assume that u and v are smooth and satisfy the standard monotonicity and concavity properties, i. e., $u' > 0$, $u'' < 0$, $v_1 > 0$, $v_2 > 0$, $v_{11} < 0$, and $v_{22} < 0$. In addition, I assume that

$$v_{12} > 0.$$

The assumption of a strictly positive cross derivative v_{12} implies that, with a rising level of fundraising, the benefactor's marginal utility from the beneficiary's net resources, $d - f$, increases. This assumption is essential for the analysis. It guarantees that fundraising has an effect not only on the extensive, but also on the intensive margin. Any rise in fundraising effort in fact prompts the benefactor to increase her donation.

If the benefactor was not bound to respond to the beneficiary's move, but *autonomously* determined both the amount donated and the level of fundraising, her most-favoured allocation would solve the maximisation problem

$$\max_{\{m \geq d \geq 0, f \geq 0\}} \quad B = u(m - d) + v(d - f, f).$$

[3] In the theatre example, straightforward interpretations of $d - f$ would be the number of additional debut performances, an increase in the quality of the cast, or comparable features induced by the donation.

The associated first-order conditions are

$$-u'(m-d)+v_1(d-f,f) \lesseqgtr 0, \quad \text{with} = 0, \text{ if } m > d > 0, \tag{3.3}$$

$$-v_1(d-f,f)+v_2(d-f,f) \leq 0, \quad \text{with} = 0, \text{ if } f > 0. \tag{3.4}$$

These conditions determine a unique allocation (d^*, f^*), which will henceforth be referred to as the benefactor's most-favoured allocation.

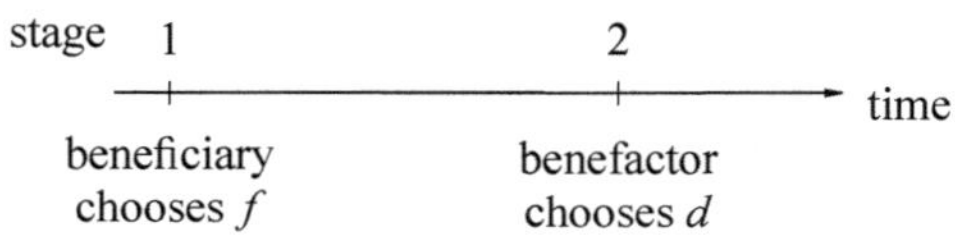

Figure 3.1: Sequence of Events

In general, however, it is not the benefactor who determines the bundle of fundraising and corresponding donation. The allocation rather is the sequential-move equilibrium of a two-stage game as depicted in Figure 3.1. First, the beneficiary chooses a level of fundraising. In reaction to the fundraising offered, the benefactor chooses an appropriate donation. This setting adopts the "power of the ask" described in the introduction, and so reflects the natural process of charitable giving.

The game is solved by backward induction. In the second stage, the benefactor observes the level of fundraising exercised, and thus maximises utility by choosing her donation d for a given f,

$$\max_{m \geq d \geq 0} \quad B = u(m-d)+v(d-f,f).$$

The first-order condition reads

$$-u'(m-d)+v_1(d-f,f) \lesseqgtr 0, \quad \text{with} = 0, \text{ if } m > d > 0. \tag{3.5}$$

Consider an interior solution. According to the implicit function theorem, the first-order condition then defines a reaction function $d = d(f)$, with

$$d'(f) = \frac{v_{11} - v_{12}}{u'' + v_{11}} > 0. \tag{3.6}$$

Hence, the donation d is an increasing function of the fundraising effort f. Equation (3.6) reveals the inevitability of a positive cross derivative. If $v_{12} \leq 0$ was possible, it would follow from (3.6) that $d'(f) < 1$. This would imply that for any additional Euro spent on fundraising, less than one Euro of additional donation would be obtained. Consequently, there would be no fundraising at all. This outcome excluded, the beneficiary anticipates the benefactor's reaction $d(f)$, and in the first stage of the game, chooses the fundraising effort f that maximises her net revenue. That is,

$$\max_{f \geq 0} \quad b = d(f) - f.$$

The first-order condition reads

$$d'(f) - 1 \leq 0 \quad \text{with} = 0, \text{ if } f > 0. \tag{3.7}$$

Consider again an interior solution. Then, equation (3.7) states that the beneficiary will choose a fundraising effort such that the last Euro spent on fundraising elicits just one additional donated Euro.

Since the reaction function $d = d(f)$ may not be concave, it cannot be ruled out that there is more than one fundraising level f that solves (3.7). However, this does not necessarily imply the existence of more than one equilibrium. The underlying argument is as follows: The beneficiary will choose the solution to (3.7) that maximises her net revenue $d - f$. If there is more than one such solution, the beneficiary is indifferent between these fundraising levels. In this case, I will assume that the beneficiary chooses the fundraising level that is advantageous for the benefactor. This assumption can be justified by the concept of so-called epsilon altruism[4]. In the context at hand, this concept implies an epsilon gain for the beneficiary in case she chooses a fundraising level that suits the benefactor. However, the gain is so small that it will not guide the beneficiary's choice over fundraising levels whenever these levels offer

[4] See, e.g., Hillier (1997, pp. 38-39).

different benefits to herself. Another argument for such an epsilon gain stems from empirical characteristics of charitable institutions. Fundraising is, in general, not an end in itself, it is more likely seen as a necessary evil by charity managers. If the beneficiary essentially dislikes fundraising in an epsilon sense, she will choose the lower of equivalent fundraising levels.

Let (d_e, f_e) define the equilibrium allocation, i. e., the solution to equations (3.6) and (3.7). Depending on the specific shape of the benefactor's utility function and on her income, the benefactor's most-favoured fundraising effort, $f*$, may be either larger than, equal to, or smaller than the equilibrium fundraising level f_e. In the first case, the benefactor is especially keen on fundraising benefits and less concerned with the resources available to the beneficiary. In the second case, there is no conflict between benefactor and beneficiary. In the the third case, a conflict between benefactor and beneficiary arises in the sense that by fundraising the beneficiary urges the benefactor to give more than she actually prefers to. In what follows, we confine attention to the case that the beneficiary bothers the benefactor.

Assumption 1. $f_e > f^*$.

This assumption is crucial in order to install what I will refer to as the beneficiary-benefactor conflict.[5] Note that Assumption 1 implies interior solutions to equations (3.5) and (3.7). Since $f^* \geq 0$, it is true that $f_e > 0$, which in turn necessitates $d_e > 0$. Besides, I claim that it is not too bold to presume that a beneficiary chooses a higher fundraising level than the benefactor prefers, since she sets f strategically to attract higher donations. Of course, the setting does not fundamentally preclude $f_e < f^*$, but I argue that the other case is the more relevant one and an economic problem of interest.

In consequence, the fundraising game ensues the following. By means of her initial choice of f, the beneficiary commits the benefactor to give a certain d. Hence, the beneficiary determines the outcome of the game, and in equilibrium, there will be an allocation with strictly higher values of d and f than in the bundle (d^*, f^*), which is preferred by the benefactor. The resulting conflict between beneficiary and benefactor is depicted in Figure 3.2.

[5] Since both f_e and f^* are endogenous, Assumption 1 may appear somewhat odd. Alternatively, I might assume that v_{12} is sufficiently large, i. e.

$$v_{12}(d^* - f^*, f^*) > -u''(m - d^*),$$

which implies $f_e > f^*$. This assumption states that, evaluated at the benefactor's bliss point, the saturation of her willingness-to-donate for fundraising proceeds more slowly than that of her utility from private consumption (which may be especially true for the wealthy).

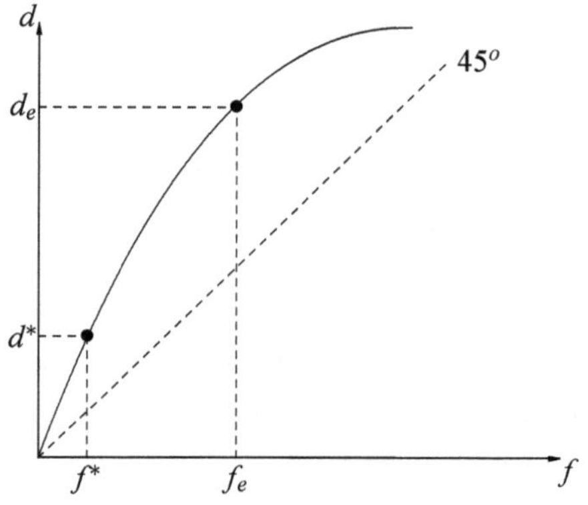

Figure 3.2: Beneficiary-Benefactor Conflict

As the following proposition states, the benefactor's most-favoured allocation is efficient whereas the equilibrium allocation is not.[6]

Proposition 1. The benefactor's most-favoured allocation (d^*, f^*) is Pareto-efficient. The equilibrium allocation (d_e, f_e) is Pareto-inefficient.

Generally, the inefficiency of the equilibrium allocation implies that the benefactor can be made better off without making the beneficiary worse off. There are viable efficiency gains that can be used to ease the beneficiary-benefactor conflict. In the following section an efficiency enhancing strategy is developped that builds on the benefactor's incentive to change the outcome of the natural fundraising process. I will address extensions to the basic model, including annoying fundraising and non-altruistic giving. Before concluding, I will turn to the very common policy of enhancing charitable donations through tax exemptions, and show that this practice may attenuate the beneficiary-benefactor conflict alongside.

3.3 Commitment to Strategic Bounteousness

Since the equilibrium of the natural fundraising game is not favourable for the benefactor, she has an incentive to search for viable strategies to overcome the beneficiary-benefactor conflict.

6 All proofs are established in the Appendix.

One possible alley would be to *credibly* commit to an upper limit, or to a precise quantity, of donations.

In order to confine the beneficiary's fundraising effort, the benefactor might establish a statutory ceiling for her philanthropic gift. This can be observed, for instance, when charitable foundations are set up. Their statutes will usually define a fixed financial endowment, and regulate the utilisation of interest profits. A suitable example might be a foundation devoted to fostering higher education and science. It may establish a fix monetary award for outstanding merits on an annual basis, appoint an objective for excess funds, and set up conditions for its conferral, such as the joint public appearance of laureate and sponsor.

As opposed to such a formal commitment, this section presents a *strategic* approach to the resolution of the beneficiary-benefactor conflict, which is motivated by the following anecdote. The former president of a German private university reported on an experience he made while approaching a potential private benefactor. He proposed to set up a meeting, on the occasion of which he would present the university, its merits and its future projects. In response, the addressee offered a five-digit Euro sum on condition that he were *not* visited.

I will demonstrate that such a strategy to limit fundraising efforts through initial bounteousness may be well-suited to ease the beneficiary-benefactor conflict.

In the sequential game as described in Section 3.2, the benefactor is bound to give d_e upon the beneficiary's offer of f_e. In order to install a more convenient allocation, the benefactor has to change behaviour. While it is common – empirically as well as in the game modelled above – that benefactors merely *react* to the fundraising activities offered by the beneficiary, I will show that the benefactor benefits from altering the agenda. In awareness of the imminent equilibrium outcome, she should initially propose some more favourable bundle (d, f) that is acceptable for the beneficiary, and so prevents the latter from enforcing (d_e, f_e).

In order to demonstrate how the allocation can be improved in this spirit, consider the indifference curves of both beneficiary and benefactor.

The set of indifference curves related to the beneficiary is defined by

$$I_b = \{(d, f) \geq 0 : d - f = const.\}.$$

This can be easily identified as the set of straight lines with slope 1 above the 45°-line in the (d, f)-space. Clearly, the beneficiary's marginal rate of substitution between d and f is given

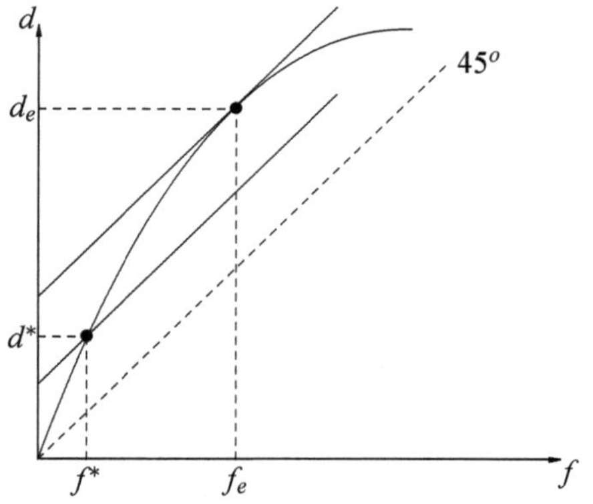

Figure 3.3: Beneficiary's Indifference Curves

by $MRS_b = 1$. That means, the beneficiary is only just willing to spend one additional Euro on fundraising in exchange for one additional donated Euro. Figure 3.3 illustrates the beneficiary's indifference curves associated with the equilibrium bundle (d_e, f_e) and the benefactor's most-favoured bundle (d^*, f^*).

The benefactor's indifference curves are defined by

$$I_B = \{(d,f) \geq 0 : u(m-d) + v(d-f,f) = const.\},$$

and the associated marginal rate of substitution between d and f reads

$$MRS_B = \frac{v_1 - v_2}{-u' + v_1}.$$

Figure 3.4 illustrates the benefactor's indifference curves, which shape up as ring-like figures around her most-favoured bundle (d^*, f^*).

Since $-u' + v_1 = 0$ holds true on the reaction curve $d = d(f)$, it follows that $MRS_B|_{d=d(f)} = \pm\infty$. That is, the benefactor's indifference curves have a vertical slope at the intersection with the reaction curve.

Since (d^*, f^*) is efficient, the beneficiary cannot be made better off without harming the benefactor. Yet, while maintaining the beneficiary's utility level derived from (d_e, f_e), the benefactor can profit by enforcing outcomes apart from those on the reaction curve.

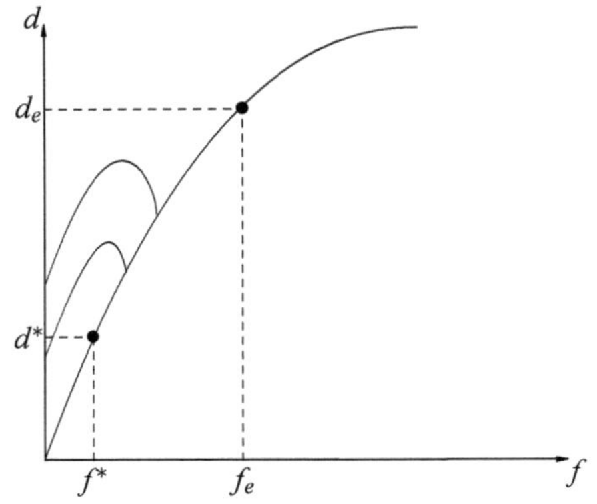

Figure 3.4: Benefactor's Indifference Curves

This is where the contemplated change of agenda comes into play. The benefactor can only avoid outcomes on the reaction curve, if she herself and not the beneficiary takes the first step. Now, the benefactor proposes a certain bundle (d, f), then the beneficiary performs the according quantity of fundraising and, finally, the benefactor effects the agreed donation.

The space of outcomes the benefactor can enforce by initially proposing a (d, f)-bundle is given by $\{(d, f) \geq 0 : d - f = d_e - f_e\}$, that is, by the beneficiary's indifference curve through $d_e - f_e$.[7] Figure 3.5 identifies the benefactor's most-favoured *feasible* bundle which is denoted by $(\hat{d}, \hat{f})$.

From the allocation $(\hat{d}, \hat{f})$, the benefactor obtains the highest utility level that is consistent with $d - f = d_e - f_e$. By proposing $(\hat{d}, \hat{f})$, the benefactor accepts to make a strictly larger contribution than she would have in response to $\hat{f}$ in the natural fundraising game.[8] The benefactor may thus be held to act in a bounteous manner. Yet, essentially, she donates more only in exchange for the beneficiary's renouncement of $f_e - \hat{f}$. I will therefore resort to the term of strategic bounteousness.

In contrast to the equilibrium outcome of the natural fundraising game, (d_e, f_e), the allocation achieved by altering the agenda, $(\hat{d}, \hat{f})$, is efficient.

7 Strictly speaking, it is the space above that parallel to the indifference curve, but the benefactor evidently prefers an allocation that lies on the lower boundary of that space.

8 Note that the equilibrium remains that of a non-cooperative game: if the benefactor were not to respond by $\hat{d} > d(\hat{f})$ to $\hat{f} < f_e$, the fundraiser would subsequently enforce (d_e, f_e).

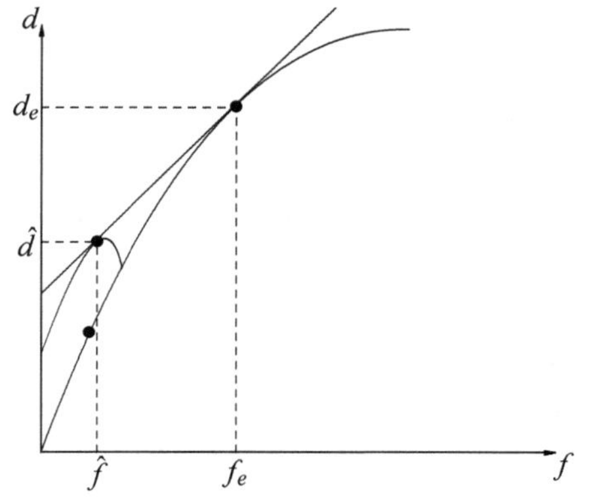

Figure 3.5: Strategic Bounteousness

Of course, it has to be noted that the institutional environment sometimes precludes the benefactor's ability to seize the agenda-setting power. Lack of information on the existence or accessibility of a philanthropic cause, for instance, prevents the contingent benefactor from anticipatorily determining the allocation. Yet, wherever potential benefactors are able to forestall the beneficiary's fundraising efforts, the following proposition holds.

Proposition 2. The benefactor's most-favoured feasible allocation $(\hat{d}, \hat{f})$ is Pareto-efficient.

So far, it has been demonstrated that fundraising in the benchmark case of the natural fundraising game is excessive compared to the benefactor's most-favoured allocation as well as to the allocation the benefactor would choose if she were able to propose outcomes on the contract curve. The following section deals with some extensions to the basic setting, especially to the case where fundraising is annoying (recall the example of an animal rights group), and to non-altruistic, or warm-glow, giving. To begin with, yet, I will outline whether the beneficiary has an incentive to repeat the fundraising game.

3.4 Extensions

3.4.1 Repeated Fundraising

The efficient outcome $(\hat{d},\hat{f})$ is enforceable in a sequential-move equilibrium whenever the benefactor succeeds in gaining agenda-setting power. However, there is no principal objection against the fundraiser's doing just so in turn, after the appointed moves have been made. Having received $\hat{d}$, and with intent to enforce a further donation, the beneficiary might opt to initiate another round of the fundraising game.

Thus, let the benefactor propose a bundle $(\hat{d},\hat{f})$, so that the beneficiary devotes some effort $\hat{f}$ to fundraising, and the benefactor donates $\hat{d}$. Does it pay off for the beneficiary to spend additional resources on fundraising? The next proposition addresses this problem.

Proposition 3. The benefactor's most-favoured feasible allocation $(\hat{d},\hat{f})$ is stable in the sense that the beneficiary has no incentive to initiate further fundraising.

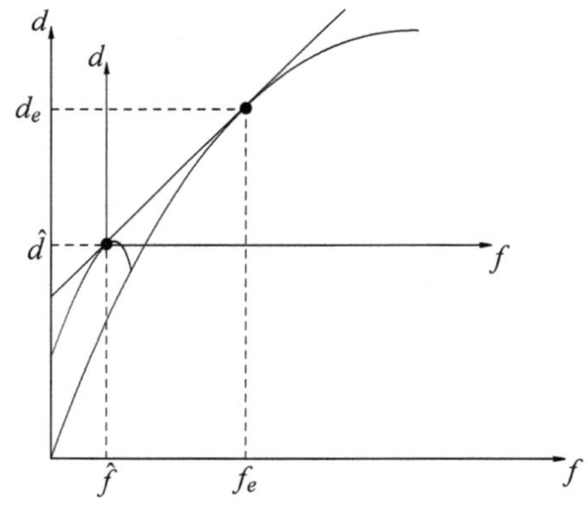

Figure 3.6: Repeated Fundraising

Figure 3.6 displays the implications of this calculus. Having reached a mutual consent in $(\hat{d},\hat{f})$, it does not pay for the beneficiary to initiate a further round of the fundraising game. The best accessible extra donation only just offsets the required additional effort.

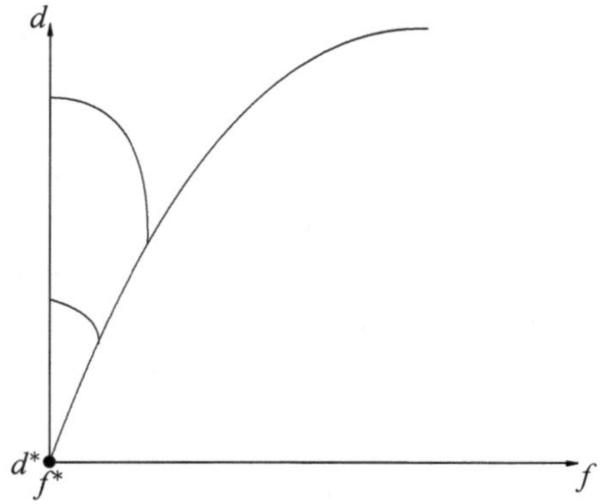

Figure 3.7: Annoying Fundraising - Benefactor's Indifference Curves

3.4.2 Annoying Fundraising

So far, it has been assumed that $v_2 > 0$, i. e., fundraising itself contributes to the welfare of the benefactor. For instance, a potential donor to a city's horticultural authority might be offered a tag to a park bench, stating her name and expressing the municipality's gratitude. Or, as in the theatre example, access to dress rehearsals helps add a private dimension to the benefactor's utility from philanthropic giving.

However, as outlined in the introduction, donations might also occur because an individual feels *coerced* upon being asked to give. Notwithstanding its role in creating positive marginal revenues, fundraising may thus have a negative impact on the benefactor's well-being. While a beggar's welfare gain, for instance, may add to the utility of a potential benefactor, the particular method of fundraising generally does not.

Thus, assume that $v_2 < 0$, while $v_{12} > 0$ continues to hold, so that the derivative of the donation function remains $d'(f) = (v_{11} - v_{12})/(u'' + v_{11}) > 0$. For $v_2 < 0$, the indifference curves of the benefactor take on a negative slope for $d > d(f)$, since

$$MRS_B = \frac{v_1 - v_2}{-u' + v_1} < 0.$$

Figure 3.7 plots the indifference curves of the benefactor. Clearly, for $v_2 < 0$ the benefactor prefers no fundraising at all. Furthermore, in Figure 3.7 it has been assumed that the benefactor does not donate at all in the absence of fundraising, making her most-favoured allocation $(d^*, f^*) = (0,0)$.

The effect of strategic bounteousness when fundraising is annoying is illustrated in Figure 3.8. The benefactor's most-favoured solution is $d^* = f^* = 0$, but the beneficiary prefers, as before, to enforce the allocation (d_e, f_e). Applying the same reasoning as in the original setting, the benefactor's best response to this conflict is to establish $(\hat{d}, 0)$, that is, to forestall any fundraising attempt by proposing the appropriate, strategically bounteous, gift. The results obtained so far shall be illustrated by the following numerical example.

Example 1. Let u be given by $u = \frac{1}{\gamma}c^\gamma$, and v by $v = \frac{1}{\gamma}b^\gamma f^\gamma - \frac{\alpha}{\gamma}f^\gamma$, where α measures the degree of annoyance experienced through fundraising activities. Assume that $m = \frac{5}{4}$. It is then readily verified that fundraising is annoying, i. e., $v_2 < 0$, as long as $\alpha > m^\gamma$. Table 3.1 provides the values for the donation, the fundraising level, and the payoffs of the benefactor and the beneficiary in the benefactor's most-favoured allocation (BMF), the equilibrium allocation (EQL), and in the benefactor's most-favoured feasible allocation (BFF) for $m = \frac{5}{4}$, $\gamma = \frac{1}{2}$, and $\alpha = \frac{4}{3}$.[9]

	d	f	B	b
BMF	0	0	2.236	0
EQL	0.750	0.500	0.236	0.250
BFF	0.250	0	2.000	0.250

Table 3.1: Example 1

This setting allows a short reference to public poverty alleviation when begging is perceived as annoying. From a sheer efficiency-oriented point of view, such policies should be designed to preempt begging by supplying an appropriate endowment from the outset. In most societies, poverty is a relevant problem, yet the public does not appreciate being confronted too openly with its existence, since it does not belong to the self-perception of an enlightened society to inadequately cope with such disadvantage. A society that values equality of opportunities, but does not appreciate being continuously reminded thereof, should act according to the

9 See the Appendix for details.

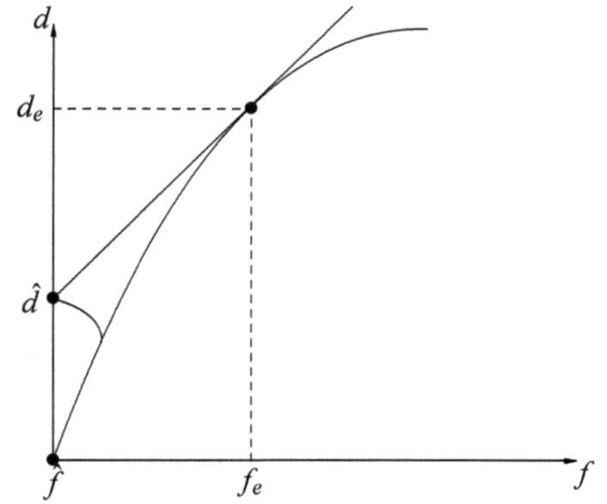

Figure 3.8: Annoying Fundraising - Strategic Bounteousness

reasoning described above. TV-reports on, or positive confrontation with the needy, and other appeals to social conscience, should thus be evaded by providing the appropriate, strategically bounteous, public poverty alleviation programme.

3.4.3 Non-altruistic Giving

The case of a non-altruistic benefactor implies a utility function of the form

$$B = u(m-d) + v(d, f) .$$

According to this setup, the benefactor is merely interested in the donation itself[10], and in fringe benefits. She does not have any specific taste for the beneficiary's net resources. Applied to the theatre example, the benefactor is interested in being mentioned in the programme leaflet, and in being admitted access to exclusive post-performance events, but not necessarily in attending newly staged performances. Moreover, she might sense a warm-glow from the sheer act of helping to maintain the theatre operations.

[10] The donation may then be motivated by the desire to experience a so-called warm-glow from giving, following, e. g., Andreoni (1990). This and other egoistic giving motives are outlined in Chapter 2.

Considering the modified utility function, the reaction function $d = d(f)$ of a non-altruistic benefactor becomes

$$d'(f) = \frac{-v_{12}}{u'' + v_{11}} > 0\,. \tag{3.8}$$

As could be expected, the donation d is an increasing function of the fundraising effort f in the non-altruistic case, too. Recall equation (3.6), where the reaction function of an altruistic benefactor is defined by $d'(f) = (v_{11} - v_{12})/(u'' + v_{11})$. In comparison, donations are less elastic with respect to fundraising effort in the case of a non-altruistic benefactor, so that the reaction function will incline more gently.

The outcome depends on the benefactor's reception of fundraising activities. If $v_2 < 0$, i. e., she dislikes fundraising, then the outcome resembles the conflict in the altruistic setting, as discussed in Section 3.4.2. Strategic bounteousness would then again imply that the benefactor offered an acceptable bundle such that the beneficiary would fully renounce from fundraising.

If, by contrast, $v_2 > 0$, meaning that the benefactor approves of suchlike treatment, she is out for more fundraising than the beneficiary is willing to offer. This setting bears the obvious problem that Assumption 1 is violated, where it is claimed that $f_e > f^*$ should hold. Anyway, since the fundraiser cannot rely on achieving $\hat{d} > d(\hat{f})$ in exchange for $\hat{f} > f_e$, she will not agree to offer any fundraising different from f_e in the first place. Strategic bounteousness is not applicable in this setting.

3.5 Tax Privilege of Donations

Beneficiary and benefactor are not the only players on the philanthropy market. Private contributions are considered a valuable source of revenue for matters of collective, societal interest. Therefore, most societies grant philanthropists tax deductibility of donations, in order to lower the price of giving and, eventually, to abate the associated externalities in a Pigouvian spirit. It will be demonstrated that such tax privileges are not only suited to foster charitable giving. They also have the potential to remedy the inefficiency associated with the beneficiary-benefactor conflict, even though this arguably is not their primary scope.

In order to incorporate the idea of a tax privilege, I assume that the government subsidises charitable giving at the marginal rate $\sigma \in [0,1]$. It covers subsidy expenditure by charging the benefactor[11] a lump-sum tax denoted by $\tau \in [0,m]$, and so maintains a balanced budget. The benefactor's utility and the government's budget may then be written as

$$B = u[m - \tau - (1-\sigma)\,d] + v(d - f, f),$$

and

$$\tau = \sigma\, d,$$

respectively. The tax load τ clearly cannot exceed the benefactor's wealth m, so that $\tau \leq m$. By construction, the game reduces to the natural setting, when $\sigma = 0$. For $\sigma < 1$, the benefactor prefers a donation that is strictly smaller than m. For $\sigma = 1$, by contrast, the benefactor faces no marginal cost of giving and, therefore will donate as much as possible. In this case, the constraint $\tau \leq m$ is binding, so that $\tau = d = m$.

The equilibrium can again be determined by backward induction. I begin by considering the case of $\sigma < 1$. Subsequently, I will turn toward the special case of a corner subsidy rate $\sigma = 1$.

In the second stage, the benefactor solves the following programme for a given structure of government intervention:

$$\max_{m \geq d \geq 0} \quad B = u[m - \tau - (1-\sigma)\,d] + v(d - f, f).$$

The first-order condition for an interior solution reads

$$-(1-\sigma)\,u'[m - \tau - (1-\sigma)\,d] + v_1(d - f, f) = 0. \tag{3.9}$$

Since $\tau = \sigma\, d$ according to the government's budget constraint, the expression reduces to

$$-(1-\sigma)\,u'(m - d) + v_1(d - f, f) = 0. \tag{3.10}$$

11 Note that analysis is restricted to the case of one representative benefactor.

This implicitly defines the donation d as a function of the fundraising level f and the marginal subsidy rate σ, that is to say, $d = d(f,\sigma)$, with

$$\frac{\partial d}{\partial f} = \frac{v_{11} - v_{12}}{(1-\sigma)\,u'' + v_{11}} > 0, \tag{3.11}$$

$$\frac{\partial d}{\partial \sigma} = \frac{-u'}{(1-\sigma)\,u'' + v_{11}} > 0. \tag{3.12}$$

In this setting, the donation does not only increase with respect to fundraising f, but also with respect to the subsidy rate σ. This applies although the subsidy generally causes both a substitution effect and an income effect. Since the income effect is neutralised by the subsidy-financing tax burden, the substitution effect predominates, so that the subsidy unambiguously fosters charitable giving.

In the first stage, the beneficiary solves

$$\max_{f \geq 0} \quad b = d - f.$$

The first-order condition for an interior solution is

$$\frac{\partial d}{\partial f} - 1 = 0,$$

which, in light of equation (3.11), can be written as

$$-v_{12}[d(f,\sigma) - f, f] - (1-\sigma)\,u''[m - d(f,\sigma)] = 0. \tag{3.13}$$

Equation (3.13) implicitly defines fundraising f as a function of the marginal subsidy rate σ, that is $f = f(\sigma)$, with

$$f'(\sigma) = -\frac{[v_{121} + (1-\sigma)\,u'''] \dfrac{\partial d}{\partial \sigma} + u''}{-v_{122} + (1-\sigma)\,u''' \dfrac{\partial d}{\partial f}}.$$

Generally, the sign of $f'(\sigma)$ cannot be unambiguously determined, as nothing has been said about the signs of the third derivatives of u and v. The fundraising level may react either positively or negatively to an increase in the subsidy of charitable gifts. In particular, the beneficiary might, on the one hand, abate her effort, because marginal fundraising is less effective in the view of a lower price of giving. On the other hand, she might even increase her effort in order to make the benefactor take full account of the lower price.[12]

The payoffs of the beneficiary and of the benefactor in the subsidy equilibrium are given by

$$b(\sigma) = d[f(\sigma),\sigma] - f(\sigma),$$
$$B(\sigma) = u[m - d(f(\sigma),\sigma)] + v[d(f(\sigma),\sigma) - f(\sigma), f(\sigma)],$$

respectively. Differentiation with respect to σ while considering the envelope theorem yields

$$b'(\sigma) = \frac{\partial d}{\partial \sigma}, \tag{3.14}$$
$$B'(\sigma) = -\frac{\sigma}{1-\sigma} v_1 \frac{\partial d}{\partial \sigma} + \left(v_2 - \frac{1}{1-\sigma} v_1 \right) f'(\sigma). \tag{3.15}$$

Following equation (3.12), the beneficiary unambiguously profits from an increase in the subsidy. The benefactor, by contrast, may either benefit or not, depending on how the beneficiary adjusts the fundraising level in response to subsidy variations.

Even if the subsidy might be of no advantage to the benefactor, this does not preclude that the subsidy will remedy the inefficiency associated with the underlying conflict. Since $b'(\sigma) > 0$, it can be inferred from (A.2) that an equilibrium with a positive subsidy rate, denoted as (d_σ, f_σ), is Pareto-efficient, if it solves

$$-u'(m - d_\sigma) + v_2(d_\sigma - f_\sigma, f_\sigma) = 0. \tag{3.16}$$

Without specifying the functions u and v, it cannot be said whether there exists a subsidy rate $\sigma \in (0,1)$ that satisfies this condition. This does not imply, however, that the question whether a Pareto-efficient subsidy equilibrium exists has to be left unanswered, because the equilibrium for the corner subsidy rate $\sigma = 1$ actually *is* efficient. For $\sigma = 1$, the benefactor seeks to give as much as possible, yet is constrained to give no more than $d = m$. Since the beneficiary will obtain $d = m$ no matter how small her fundraising effort, she will consequently choose $f = 0$. Obviously, the allocation $(d = m, f = 0)$ is Pareto-efficient. It can thus be stated:

[12] A related discussion has been triggered by Andreoni and Payne (2003, 2011), who theoretically and empirically examined effects of government *grants* on fundraising. The results imply that such an intervention will significantly reduce fundraising. If, to a beneficiary, private donations are a perfect substitute for government grants, fundraising should respond likewise in the wake of a subsidisation policy that strictly increases giving.

Proposition 4. There exists at least one marginal subsidy rate $\sigma^* \in (0,1]$ such that the resulting subsidy equilibrium $(d_{\sigma^*}, f_{\sigma^*})$ is Pareto-efficient.

Of course, the equilibrium with a corner subsidy rate leads to an extreme allocation, but it is possible, theoretically. The benefactor's wealth is completely merged into her tax burden, and the rebate is just large enough to permit a donation of $d = m$. Other potential subsidy equilibria depend on the specification of the utility function, as shall be illustrated by the following numerical example.

Example 2. Let $v = \frac{1}{\gamma} b^\gamma f^\gamma$, and u defined as in Example 1. Assume that $m = \frac{5}{4}$. Table 3.2 provides the values for the donation, the fundraising level, the payoffs of the benefactor and the beneficiary, and the subsidy rate in various allocations for $\gamma = \frac{1}{2}$ and $\gamma = 1$, respectively.[13] BMF denotes the benefactor's most-favoured allocation, EQL denotes the equilibrium allocation, i. e., the equilibrium with $\sigma = 0$, SUB denotes an efficient subsidy equilibrium with $\sigma^* \in (0,1)$, and COS denotes the subsidy equilibrium with the corner subsidy rate $\sigma^* = 1$.

		d	f	B	b	σ^*
	BMF	0.250	0.125	2.250	0.125	–
$\gamma = \frac{1}{2}$	EQL	0.750	0.500	2.121	0.250	–
	SUB	1.125	0.125	1.414	1.000	0.875
	COS	1.250	0	0	1.250	1
	BMF	0	0	1.250	0	–
$\gamma = 1$	EQL	1.250	1	0.250	0.250	–
	SUB_1	1.250	0.625	0.391	0.625	0.375
	SUB_2	1.250	0.250	0.250	1	0.750
	COS	1.250	0	0	1.250	1

Table 3.2: Example 2

As can be taken from Table 3.2, there is more than one efficient subsidy equilibrium with an interior subsidy rate for $\gamma = 1$.[14] For $\sigma^* = 0.375$, both the beneficiary *and* the

[13] See the Appendix for details. Note that $u'' = 0$, $v_{11} = 0$, and $v_{22} = 0$ if $\gamma = 1$. This, however, does not impair the example, as the model is still well-behaved in the sense that it generates distinctive allocations.

[14] In fact, there are infinitely many such equilibria, as each subsidy equilibrium with $\sigma \in [0.375, 1]$ is efficient. See the Appendix for details.

benefactor benefit from a tax privilege of donations that enforces an efficient allocation, whereas $\sigma^* = 0.750$ favours solely the beneficiary. For $\gamma = \frac{1}{2}$ there is only one interior subsidy equilibrium. This outcome turns out to be advantageous for the beneficiary relative to the equilibrium without a tax privilege, but makes the benefactor worse off.

It has been demonstrated in Sections 3.3 and 3.5 that both a commitment of the benefactor to strategic bounteousness and a tax privilege of donations have the potential to remedy the inefficiency associated with the beneficiary-benefactor conflict. Either strategy results in a Pareto-efficient allocation. However, the bundles $(d_{\sigma^*}, f_{\sigma^*})$ and $(\hat{d}, \hat{f})$ differ with respect to the distribution of welfare between the beneficiary and the benefactor.

Proposition 5. The beneficiary strictly prefers the allocation $(d_{\sigma^*}, f_{\sigma^*})$. The benefactor strictly prefers the allocation $(\hat{d}, \hat{f})$.

The following example illustrates how subsidisation and strategic bounteousness change the outcome relative to the benchmark allocation (d_e, f_e), and whom the efficiency gains accrue to.

Example 3. Consider the specification of the model outlined in Example 2. Table 3.3 provides the values for the donation, the fundraising level, and the payoffs of the benefactor and the beneficiary in the benefactor's most-favoured allocation (BMF), the equilibrium allocation (EQL), an efficient subsidy equilibrium (SUB) with $\sigma^* \in (0,1)$, and the benefactor's most-favoured feasible allocation (BFF) for $m = \frac{5}{4}$ and $\gamma = \frac{1}{2}$.[15]

	d	f	B	b	σ^*
BMF	0.250	0.125	2.250	0.125	–
EQL	0.750	0.500	2.121	0.250	–
SUB	1.125	0.125	1.414	1.000	0.875
BFF	0.450	0.200	2.236	0.250	–

Table 3.3: Example 3

15 See the Appendix for details.

The beneficiary mainly reaps the efficiency gains associated with subsidising charitable giving. The benefactor, by contrast, may even be worse off in the subsidy equilibrium than in the natural fundraising equilibrium, as the benefactor's utility may be decreasing in the subsidy rate.

3.6 Concluding Remarks

This chapter provides a model of the common fundraising process in the sense that it incorporates the "power of the ask", the notion that benefactors generally do not give but upon request. The fundamental assumption driving the argument is that a beneficiary, with intent to enforce higher donations, strategically initiates more fundraising than is favourable for the benefactor. If one is willing to accept this presupposition, a conflict evolves between the benefactor and the beneficiary regarding the extent of fundraising activities.

With the "ask" in power, the beneficiary determines the outcome of the process, and the resulting allocation is obviously not efficient. A Pareto-optimal allocation can be implemented by a mechanism I refer to as strategic bounteousness. The idea is to forestall the beneficiary's move by proposing a more favourable bundle of giving and fundraising that is, however, consistent with the beneficiary's objective of net revenue maximisation.

This implies that the natural fundraising process is altered. Evidently, this point raises the discussion whether that is at all possible: Is the "ask" *necessarily* in force, and if it is, why so? If individuals do not actually express an existing taste for giving, this might be due to an information problem, for instance. Either they simply do not know whereto or how to proceed their gift. Or they freeride, until social pressure - embodied by the fundraising instance - becomes too heavy. In the first case, there is little chance to change the agenda. In the second, though, a potential benefactor should anticipate the conflict, and respond through strategic bounteousness.

The strategy of limiting fundraising in order to implement an efficient allocation straightforwardly extends to the cases of annoying fundraising and of warm-glow giving. Beside the decentral mechanism, the fundraising conflict can be alleviated through the common policy of granting donations tax privileges. While the latter mechanism mainly benefits the fundraiser, strategic bounteousness enables the benefactor to incorporate the inherent efficiency gains.

While analysis is restricted to different structures of the benefactor's utility function, another obvious extension of the model would be to address the effect of competition on the relevance of the beneficiary-benefactor conflict. In the setting at hand, however, I confine attention to a monopolistic fundraiser. The benefactor, representing the whole range of potential donors in the society, acts as a price taker when responding to the beneficiary's choice. This setting appears realistic when it comes to, e. g., religious institutions such as churches, which are in general not readily substitutable among each other. For relief organisations, by contrast, perceptible differentiation is much more difficult to achieve. Here it would be more reasonable to assume oligopolistic or perfect competition, which would make the inefficiency gradually disappear.

Another extension would be to analyse implications on the design of fundraising strategies. The central concern for the beneficiary, or charity manager, should be to enable the benefactor to propose an allocation, i. e., to resort to a form of strategic bounteousness. Consider a scheme, where different donation levels are linked to corresponding levels of available prestige[16], or to specific fundraising activities, and where these allocations lie on the contract curve. The beneficiary informs the benefactor about this scheme, and the latter chooses her donation according to one of the allocations offered. Except for the case where the act of informing the benefactor is already perceived as excessive fundraising, this scheme is equivalent to initial bounteousness if it is appropriately designed.

[16] Consider the publication scheme in Harbaugh (1998a), for instance, where donors are grouped to different categories according to which bracket of donations they choose. The donor's names are then announced together with the corresponding category, which may range from, e. g., "friendly supporter" to "patron".

4 An Empirical Investigation of Donor-Fundraiser Interaction

"It is not typically possible [...] to match firm-level data to household-level data on contributions." Sonia H. Manzoor, John D. Straub (2005, p. 463).

Private donations usually do not occur if not distinctly solicited. So, fundraising is introduced as an intermediate process. The resulting donor-fundraiser interaction displays a complex exchange of resources. Both the donor's and the fundraiser's utility are affected by the charitable cause itself, so that costly solicitation has a negative impact in the first instance. However, the donor may not only profit from a sense of warm glow, but may even savour fringe benefits associated with fundraising. This chapter integrates two extensive datasets on the donor and on the charity level, respectively, and empirically assesses the ambiguous impact of fundraising on charitable giving, while emphasising the relevance of donor convictions.

4.1 Motivation

While the effect of fundraising on the decision to donate to a charitable instance is widely acknowledged as unambiguously positive, the impact of fundraising effort on the decision of *how much* to sacrifice, is theoretically and empirically unclear. At first glance, fundraising is unfavourable to both donor and recipient, because it deteriorates the effectivity of the gift in terms of cause-orientation. But apart from this relation, fundraising may exhibit additional effects on the donor; it may be regarded as pleasant, as in case of charity-dinners, or may be sensed as unsettling.[1]

The phenomenon that donations only occur upon solicitation is known, and has been presented earlier, as the "power of the ask". However, fundraising generally goes beyond simply asking for gifts. Typically, it involves a more complex exchange of resources between beneficiary and benefactor, especially concerning the donor's utility from the provision process. The fundraiser, consequently, may face a trade-off between adding revenue from an additional contributor, and losing revenue from some other contributors due to their potential aversion to fundraising expenditures. Because of these ambiguous effects, overall contributions are likely to be a nonlinear function of fundraising expenditures.

Since private donations usually do not occur if not distinctly solicited, many instances excercise fundraising activities of some sort. In the remainder of this chapter, I will resort to the term of fundraising in the following sense.

Fundraising. Every measure or institution dedicated to the solicitation, administration, and transmission of charitable gifts.

In the case of (nonprofit) charitable organisations, fundraising effort naturally translates to the entirety of expenditures that are not immediately dedicated to the statutory charitable cause. This usually comprises costs of advertisement, solicitation, and administration.

As outlined in the previous chapters, theoretical models of the philanthropy market differ in which role they assign to fundraising in the process of charitable giving. One important group of models explains the apparent indispensability of fundraising with its capacity to lower potentially prohibitive transaction costs. These costs can be due to lack of information, or may result from obstacles to conveying the gift to the intended recipient, among others.

1 For a theoretical assessment of these ambiguous fundraising effects, see Chapter 3, and von Kotzebue and Wigger (2008).

Donors are made aware of philathropic causes they might never have come to know, or they are reminded of causes they already decided to support before. Fundraising institutions can also be helpful when it comes to informing voluntary contributors on the progress of reaching some threshold supply of a collective good in the presence of non-convexities. Besides, donors usually do not dispose of the means or skills that are frequently needed to guarantee a correct transaction of the gift. The legal and institutional framework, the political situation in crisis zones, or regional particularities in general, pose likely challenges. This argument is adapted in models that emphasise fixed costs and transaction costs, as in Andreoni (1998), Andreoni and Payne (2003), Vesterlund (2003), Bag and Roy (2008), and Shang and Croson (2009).[2]

Another group of models addresses mechanisms employed by charitable institutions in order to enhance private giving. Raffle models, as presented by Morgan (2000), Morgan and Sefton (2000), and Duncan (2002), demonstrate the effect of linking donations to the opportunity of gaining private utility by winning a lottery prize. Other approaches, as in Glazer and Konrad (1996), Harbaugh (1998a,b), Romano and Yildirim (2001), and Bac and Bag (2003), emphasise the role of publishing the benefactor's name in conjunction with the amount given. Thus, fundraisers choose strategies that add a private dimension to the causes supported by the gift – either immediately through a raffle, or more indirectly, through gift announcements.

Empirical assessments of the charity market are largely concentrated on measuring the crowding effect of government grants on voluntary contributions to collective causes. While purely altruistic giving motives would suggest total crowding-out, the empirical evidence in more and more sophisticated analyses over the past decades gives a more differentiated picture.[3] Relating to this chapter's focus, the most important recent contribution in this field is made by Andreoni and Payne (2003, 2011). Their approach is to incorporate the behavioural response of fundraising to government grants into the crowd-out estimation, and the results suggest that a considerable part of the effect is due to reductions in fundraising (which shows not only the indispensable role of fundraising in attracting gifts, but also just how much charities dislike this part of their business).[4]

---

2 A broader overview is given in Chapter 2, and in von Kotzebue and Wigger (2010).

3 See, e. g., Steinberg (1991), Auten et al. (2002), Ribar and Wilhelm (2002), Eckel et al. (2005), Karlan and List (2007). An overview is, again, given in von Kotzebue and Wigger (2010).

4 The study estimates that for each $ 10,000 of annual government grants, nonprofits cut fundraising by $ 1,370, and private donations are reduced by about $ 7,271. Depending on the type of organisation, the crowd-out due to lower fundraising is found to range between 42 and 73%, or between 80 and 132% of total crowd-out.

An explanation for this strong sensitivity of fundraising to alternative revenue sources also lies in the presence of charity watchdog institutions that play an important role in conveying trustworthiness of nonprofit organisations, and that define standards of best practice. A "good" ratio of cause-related expenditures to costs of fundraising and administration can be a substantial advantage in the increasingly competitive charity market. Estimations suggest that total annual donations in Germany are pretty much constant, around 4.5 - 5 bn Euros, and that their relative change, adjusted for extraordinary giving occasions such as disasters, tends to fall behind the trend in disposable income.[5] In an attempt to develop their market share, though, charities suffer high expenses when attracting new donors. These may amount to 100 - 200 Euros per effective donor, contrasted by an expected initial donation of around 50 Euros, and a follow-up rate of merely around 50%. In consequence, nonprofit organisations are very reactive to an easing of their budget constraint through government grants.

The empirical literature does not only reflect the influence of rules of best practice in the cited crowd-out measures, but also in estimations of the return to fundraising. Charities generally appear to renounce net revenue maximisation.[6] Andreoni and Payne (2011), for instance, report estimates that imply receipts of over five dollars for the marginal dollar worth of fundraising effort.

The disparity between the generally high overall return to fundraising and that when soliciting new donors hints at the crucial role that donor *commitment* plays for a charity's sustainable prosperity. Tying prior donors to the organisation is the only way to raise money while keeping the fundraising-to-expenditures ratio appropriately low. In this light, it becomes obvious to examine in greater detail the ambiguous relation of fundraising and giving, especially when it comes to repeated solicitations.

There is a vast toolbox that is widely used to enhance donor commitment, ranging from simple follow-up telefone calls to appealing events. Several organisations send birthday cards, the nature preservation organisation WWF offers welcome packages in some countries, including access to their website's members area, and UNICEF invites supporters to cinema previews related to child relief. Yet, fundraising professionals are aware of the fact that repeatedly addressing their donors obviously bears the risk of annoying or even alienating them. It depends mainly on individual preferences – essentially unobservable to the charity – whether the effort

5 Cf. DZI (2010), p. 352.
6 See, e. g., Weisbrod and Dominguez (1986), Weisbrod (1988, 1998), Khanna et al. (1995).

is appreciated, or not. There are few forms of commitment that combine steady revenues for the organisation with little nuisance for the donor. A case in point is the sponsorship contract that guarantees regular support for, e. g., one particular needy child, and that is increasingly adopted by the relevant organisations. What is more, fundraising in the form of periodic information on the development of the supported child is most likely to even *enhance* donor commitment.

In empirical studies that investigate this complex donor-fundraiser relation, a convincing link of individual-level data on donor motivation to nonprofit financial data is desirable, yet difficult to achieve. Household-level surveys hardly ever include the particular beneficiary, are restricted to donations to a specific type of charity, or lack important socio-demographic control variables such as disposable income. Individual tax returns give vast information on important donor characteristics, yet none on the recipient, and none on non-filed gifts.[7] On the other hand, organisation-level data naturally are aggregated beyond the scope of a single gift, and therewith generally do not include donor characteristics, or the particular fundraising measure that entailed a gift.

Consequently, empirical investigations that address the strategic interaction of donor and fundraiser on the basis of individual donors or gifts, are rare to date.[8] Kingma (1989), and Manzoor and Straub (2005) constitute a benchmark in the literature because they plausibly match household-level contributions to radio stations with station-level data on revenue, including revenue from government grants.

This chapter contributes to the literature by integrating much broader data on both sides of the nonprofit market, namely by assigning individual donations to the fundraising effort of the corresponding organisation. The dataset allows to make use of fundraising measures on the aggregate level as well as on the individual level, and link them to a specific donation. The household-level survey offers several individual control variables, notably on income, household size, education, region, and age, among others.

The merged dataset, based on individual donations, suggests three different measures of an organisation's fundraising effort, (1) the fundraising share in total annual expenditures, (2) an approximation of total annual fundraising expenditures and (3) an approximation of the

7 For a study using the German Taxpayer Panel, see Borgloh (2008).

8 See, e. g., Kingma (1989), Khanna et al. (1995), Straub (1999), Manzoor and Straub (2005). A theoretical approach to strategic donor-fundraiser interaction is proposed in Chapter 3, for instance.

fundraising intensity the individual encounters, all of which will be described in further detail in Section 4.2. For now, an introductory overview is given as follows:

- Characteristics of the merged dataset
  - Number of observations: 34,860 individual gifts;
  - Households (5,307): giftsize, addressee, date, giving motivation, fundraising measure encountered, net income, socio-demographic controls;
  - Organisations (149): Resource structure, fundraising share, purpose;
- Objective: grasp determinants of charitable giving, with a special focus on the influence of fundraising effort.

In assessing the effect of fundraising on charitable gifts, it is crucial to distinguish between the effect on the extensive margin and that on the intensive margin.[9] The former indicates the influence of solicitation on the fundamental decision of *whether* to donate, or not, and is recognised as unambiguously positive in the literature and by fundraising professionals. In order to produce revenue from private contributions at all, nonprofits need to address potential donors in the first place. The fundraising effect on the intensive margin, by contrast, denominates the impact on the subordinate decision of *how much* to give. As indicated above, this effect is by far more vague. Depending on individual characteristics and on the method employed, an increased effort may result in higher, lower, or even in terminated giving. The dataset employed in this chapter restricts analysis to the intensive margin, since it is built on executed gifts, and therewith systematically precludes events of ineffective fundraising.

Since a major part of the work on this chapter was dedicated to merging the two datasets, much of the remainder will describe the characteristics of the obtained, unique, dataset, before presenting estimation results that investigate donor-fundraiser interaction on the charity market in Germany.

The results plausibly confirm that fundraising effort has a negative impact on donations on the intensive margin. Furthermore, gifts prove highly sensitive to a donor's convictions toward charitable giving. The coefficients of interest are robust to several specifications, especially to the fundraising measures employed. One of them is based on the donor's perception of fundraising, whereas the other two are derived from the charities' financial data.

9 This distinction leans on Andreoni and Payne (2003).

The remainder of the chapter is organised as follows. I will continue with a more detailed description of the underlying datasets and the merging process in Section 4.2, and describe basic manipulations necessary to tackle methodical concerns due to the characteristics of the dataset in Section 4.3.1. Subsequently, the estimation results will be outlined in Section 4.3.2. The chapter closes with some concluding remarks in Section 4.4.

4.2 Data Description

This chapter builds on the integration of two extensive datsets, one of which covers the donor, the other the charitable organisation side of the philanthropy market in Germany. While households in the GfK Charity Scope are chosen so as to be representative of the German population, the panel of charities covers all those organisations that report their figures to the DZI, a charity watchdog organisation. Since donors in the former set are asked to state the addressee of their every particular gift, the associated information on individual and gift-related characteristics can be matched with data on the addressee's fundraising effort.

The datasets display considerable overlap that can be exploited to empirically assess the donor-fundraiser-relation in that way. Yet, the merging process entails a bias toward the - so to say - *institutionalised* philanthropy market: by construction, the data are restricted to information on gifts to well-established charitable organisations - and not on those to individuals or smaller entities such as neighborhood associations, or animal shelters. These limitations will be examined in more detail later in this section, after the basic characteristics of the two datasets have been described.[10]

4.2.1 The GfK Charity Scope

The GfK is a private corporation that provides quantitative market research and consulting in various industry branches, and by the same token conducts a large survey on charitable giving. This so-called GfK Charity Scope is a representative panel of 10,781 households, covering 140,747 single donations in the years 2004 through 2010. Its core intent is to provide insight into the impact of fundraising measures, and to explore potentials for target-oriented fundraising. In this light, the survey raises information not only on the size, but also on the

[10] In the remainder of the chapter, I will mark raw, unmodified variables from the two original datasets by using `typewriter` font.

addressee and the concomitant circumstances of the gift, on socio-demographic characteristics of the donor, and on her motivation. The GfK Charity Scope reports 25 entries for every giving event, and can be summarised in the following first overview:

- Basic characteristics: 140,747 giving events, 10,781 respondents, period 2004 - 2010;
- Distribution of gifts over time: 2004: 12,115, 2005: 23,150, 2006: 21,226, 2007: 20,232, 2008: 20,676, 2009: 21,495, 2010: 21,853;
- Respondents identified by `household number` (1), donations additionally by `year` (2), `month` (3), `day` (4);
- Socio-demographic characteristics
  - Categorical variables: `region` (5), `gender` (6), `education level` (7), `social status` (8), `occupation` (9);
  - Numerical variables: `size of residential city` (10), `age of respondent` (11), `household income` (12; monthly, net, Euros), `household size` (13), `number of children` (14; <14 years);
- Donation-related characteristics
  - Categorical variables: `type of addressee` (15), `type of gift` (16), `sponsorship` (17), `inducement to give` (18), `timing of gift` (19), `type of relief org.` (20), `addressee` (21; four-digit code; values: 48, otherwise hand-written entry), `nature of in-kind gift` (22), `fundraising` (23; values: 22, otherwise hand-written entry), `mode of payment` (24);
  - Numerical variables: `size of gift` (25; Euros).

In the further process of manipulating the dataset, three of the original variables are omitted. First, I do not consider `social status` (8) a suitably well-defined parameter. It is not quite clear what it actually measures, especially in delimitation to the combined indication of income, education level, and occupation. Alongside, this results in a considerable risk of multicollinearity in estimation procedures. Second, the dataset is restricted to monetary gifts, because in-kind donations are not easily approximated in terms of value, and treating them as zero entries neither correctly assesses their impact. This naturally entails the elimination of the variables `type of gift` (16) and `nature of in-kind gift` (22). The concentration on monetary donations reduces the number of giving events to 130,744 observations, or by 7.11%.

Besides, the variable `education` is modified in order to ease interpretation. The nine education-levels are such grouped, that the resulting classes respond to education quartiles. The variables `income`, `age`, and `city size` are evaluated at their class means. Even in the case of the highly influential variable `income`, this is quite innocuous, since the classes merely span 250 Euros.

Table 4.1 gives summary statistics of the numerical variables in the household dataset.

Table 4.1: GfK Charity Scope: Summary Statistics

	mean	sd	median	p25, p75
Giftsize[1)]	27.4072	65.5377	20	10, 30
HH income[2)]	2556.44	1354.20	2375	1625, 3125
Age[2)]	46.4172	18.6607	47	32, 62
HH size[2)]	2.4784	1.1849	2	2, 3
Children[2)]	0.3510	0.7215	0	0, 0
City size[2)]	256,889	515,397	35,000	7,500, 150,000

Number of observations: 1) *130,744* (monetary gifts), 2) *10,781* (households).

Although it builds on a fixed set of respondents, the GfK Charity Scope's useability as a panel is, by construction, restricted. Each of the 10,781 households receives a questionnaire every month indeed, yet fills it in and sends it back only in case a gift has *effectively been made* during the precedent month. Much of the information involved (such as the addressee, the motivation to give, or the fundraising measure encountered) pertains to the single event, and so potentially varies on a daily basis. Other important parameters, notably household income, are related to the respondent rather than to the gift, and so vary on a month-to-month basis at the most. In order to ensure that no information on the single donation be lost, an actual household panel hence would have to be constructed on a *daily* basis, which would obviously make no sense given the negligible share of non-zero entries in then roughly 27 m observations. Referring to a monthly or even a yearly basis would corrode most of the essential variation, especially when it comes to important index variables (such as, again, the inducement to give to the specific cause, or the fundraising action encountered), which obviously cannot be averaged over time, or over households, in a sensible way. Apart from that, any aggregation would raise questions on how to replace missing values, since a zero gift may be due to either ineffective or simply no fundraising at all.[11] Hence, in the analysis to come, the GfK Charity Scope is treated as a seven-year cross-sectional *gift-level* dataset, and resort to cluster-robust estimation techniques in order to address differences in individual giving frequency within years.

4.2.2 The DZI Spenden-Almanach

The organisation-level data are provided by the Deutsches Zentralinstitut für soziale Fragen (DZI). The DZI is a research institute and charity watchdog organisation that issues an annual publication on the scope of activity and the financial figures of charitable organisations in Germany. This so-called DZI Spenden-Almanach features a panel of 289 charities that qualify for the DZI-Spendensiegel[12], a seal of approval that is intended to indicate sound financial conduct, and therewith trustworthiness, of charitable organisations. It reports total annual revenues, annual gifts revenues, and the fundraising share in total expenditures, 2004 through 2008. An important share of the charities operating in Germany is covered by the dataset: in 2008, the gifts revenues of the DZI-organisations amounted to roughly 1.6 bn Euros, while a cautious projection by the institute suggests monetary gifts worth 4.5 bn Euros in Germany for the same year.[13] On the whole, the DZI dataset delivers six variables that are conducive to the focus of this chapter, as can be taken from the following introductory overview:

- Basic characteristics: 289 charitable organisations, period 2004 - 2008;
- 1,217 organisation years (consistent with 4.211 observations per charity);
- Observations identified by `addressee` (1; four-digit code), `year` (2);
- Categorical variables: `type of organisation` (3), `fundraising share` (4);

[11] Since not every participant donates every month or even every year, many "observations" would need to be created by stating a zero gift and predicting the missing entries for the fundraising method encountered, among many others. Unfortunately, even predicting these unsuccessful efforts is impossible since the dataset is restricted to events of *effective* fundraising. Quite clearly, designing the questionnaire to be answered independently of whether a gift was made or not, would solve this problem.

[12] Henceforth DZI-organisations.

[13] cf. Wilke (2010), p. 6.

- Numerical variables: `total annual revenues` (5; Euros), `annual gifts revenues` (6; Euros).

The DZI-publication is directed towards private donors that seek information on purpose and financial conduct of charitable organisations. Depending on the specific cause supported, the fundraising share may vary without indicating differences in the quality of administration. For instance, it is less costly to raise money for needy children than for many other causes. Concerns that the exact fundraising share might be misleading for potential donors thus entail a policy of somewhat reducing information on this key figure. Accordingly, the DZI-organisations are assigned to three categories, depending on whether their fundraising share is considered "low" ($< 10\%$), "appropriate" ($< 20\%$), or "justifiable" ($\leq 35\%$).[14] Six charities report zero fundraising in at least one of the years covered by the dataset.

Another limitation of the dataset is that, by the same argument, no numbers are available for absolute fundraising expenditures. I employ an approximation that relates the class mean of the fundraising share to total annual *revenues*. The underlying assumption is that, by definition, expenditures are very closely tied to revenues in the nonprofit sector. All expenditures that do not contribute to the charitable cause are entirely subsumed under the category of fundraising, so that total revenues are exactly balanced by the entirety of statutory and fundraising-related expenditures.[15]

As Table 4.2 shows, the gap between total expenditures and total revenues of the DZI-organisations is in fact small, overall. Referring to the period the dataset covers, the average ratio lies at 0.9629, which entails a slight overstatement of fundraising expenditures when employing total revenues instead of total expenditures in the approximation. The ratio even amounts to 0.9996 for 2001 - 2008, when excluding 2004 and 2005. The year 2005 deviates considerably from the overall record in that revenues increased by substantially more than expenditures did. The boost in revenues is likely to be only partly due to the rising number

[14] Organisations that continuously report fundraising shares of over 30% of their annual expenditures are subject to a case-specific inspection of whether an efficient and parsimonious disposition of funds might be ensured anyway.

[15] Precisely, the DZI distinguishes between three subcategories of expenditures: immediately statute-related expenditures, fundraising expenditures, and administration expenditures. Their measure of fundraising share relates cumulated fundraising and administration expenditures to total expenditures. This is in line with the notion of fundraising presented in Chapter 3, that comprises *all* costs necessary to collect and convey the donation, and with the definition in Section 4.1. Wherever fundraising expenditures are mentioned henceforth, the term implicitely indicates the sum of fundraising and administration expenditures.

Table 4.2: DZI-organisations: Financial Data

	2004	2005	2006	2007	2008
DZI-org.[1)]	223	230	236	253	270
Total exp.	2,311,649,683	2,764,850,561	2,628,595,418	2,996,001,978	3,084,791,009
Total rev.	2,455,411,853	3,157,787,020	2,579,430,627	2,996,138,738	3,153,164,412
Exp./rev.[2)]	0.9415	0.8756	1.0191	1.0000	0.9783
Assets	2,721,392,556	3,292,586,265	3,226,976,158	3,413,190,763	3,684,247,206
Frs./exp.[3)]	16.1	13.9	13.0	13.6	13.8

1) 2002: *187*, 2003: *200*; 2) 2001: 1.0119, 2002: 0.9848, 2003: 1.0033;
3) Average fundraising share (%) as reported by DZI. 2001: 15.5, 2002: 15.3, 2003: 15.8.

of DZI-organisations. The development in 2006, where revenues sank again despite a further increase in organisations, and the overall development in the organisations' assets point in another direction. In 2005, extraordinary donations in the wake of the Southeast Asia Tsunami resulted in revenues significantly above the underlying trend. The same effect applies to 2004, yet to a weaker extent, since the Tsunami occurred very late in that year, on December 26th. A fraction of this unprecedented additional giving was obviously devoted to financial consolidation.

Besides, another striking development is likely to result from the disaster: significantly lower fundraising shares after 2004 indicate that the impressive degree of devastation – and its extensive media coverage – attracted numerous *new* donors, and therewith in a sense disburdened the organisations from this relatively costly task. A considerable fraction of those donors was thereupon accessible by means of relatively inexpensive follow-up measures, reducing the expenditures on otherwise necessary, and relatively ineffective, blind solicitations.

Table 4.3: DZI-organizations: Summary Statistics

	mean	sd	median	p25, p75
Gifts rev.	6,468,898	18,756,270	4,897,491	1,435,129, 23,802,710
Total rev.	17,058,890	54,732,530	9,532,466	2,360,701, 66,080,730
Frs. share[1)]	0.1281	0.0863	0.15	0.05, 0.15

Number of observations: *1,217*.
2004: *223*, 2005: *230*, 2006: *236*, 2007: *253*, 2008: *270*.
1) Fundraising share computed from class means.

So, employing revenues instead of expenditures in my measure of fundraising expenditures is rather innocuous. Inaccuracy is more likely due to the use of class means in place of the exact fundraising share. The measure slightly understates fundraising, on average, as can be taken from the summary statistics of the organisation-level dataset presented in Table 4.3. Yet, the distribution is right-skewed, as indicated by the median of 0.15, and in the process of merging the datasets, most of the zero-fundraising organisations will show to drop out.[16]

Gifts revenues and, even more so, total revenues display a right-skewed distribution, implying that the charity market is to some extent concentrated on relatively few very large organisations. The average fundraising share obtained over class means understates the figure given by the DZI (14.1918, an organisation-weighted average 2004 through 2008). This hints at the fact that the actual fundraising shares tend to be biased towards the upper boundary of the respective class (whereas my measure implicitely assumes an equal distribution within classes).

4.2.3 The Merged Charity Market Dataset

The assessment at hand of the charity market in Germany is essentially built on the approach to merge data on individual donors with those on organisations. The GfK Charity Scope offers this opportunity, because it requests the survey participants to reveal the addressee of their respective donation. So, individual giving attitudes can be set into relation with basic characteristics of the receiving organisation.[17]

It cannot be taken for granted, of course, that general financial conduct, e. g. overall fundraising expenditures, have a substantial influence on an individual's giving behaviour. Yet, donors are increasingly well informed, and the case of the German Committee for UNICEF shows that they react very senstively to fundraising shares perceived as excessive.[18] Besides, the dataset includes a donation-related measure of fundraising as a control.

The merging process was conducted over the combined match of the variables `addressee` and `year` in both datasets, therewith assigning to every individual donation the correspond-

[16] One large organisation will remain, reporting zero expenditures on fundraising (and administration) in 2007.

[17] For some detail on the rather laborious merging procedure, see Appendix B.

[18] In 2007, UNICEF's payments to external consultants were subject to extensive media coverage, and an emotional debate on fundraising shares. Gifts revenues sank from 87,184,085.12 (2003) and 92,005,437.31 (2004) to 58,503,968.89 (2008), according to the figures reported by DZI. In 2006 and 2007, the organisation was not awarded a DZI-Spendensiegel. 2005 saw a doubling of donations due mainly to the Tsunami.

ing set of annual organisation-based variables from the DZI-panel. The following overview summarises the basic characteristics of the merged dataset:

- Matching conjointly over `addressee` and `year`, period 2004 - 2008 ;
- 5,307 (10,781) households, 34,860 (140,747) monetary donations (consistent with 6.5687 observations per household over five years);
- 149 (289) organisations.

Concentrating on donations to DZI-organisations means to exclude roughly half of the donors, and three quarters of the donations. However, a large fraction of donations (43,348) is lost, because the DZI-data only reach until 2008, whereas GfK-households are tracked until 2010. This taken into account, 35.8% of all GfK-donations are directed towards DZI-organisations, and hence survive the matching process. The restriction to DZI-organisations entails a selection bias towards well-established charities. It also includes many of those that are especially dependent on trust, either due to heavy competition on their submarket, or because they operate in fields rather intransparent for an individual donor, for instance in overseas famine relief. The clearly predominant type of nonprofits in the dataset is the relief organisation, while such with a cultural or ecological scope are not well represented, as put out in Table 4.4. When sub-dividing relief organisations, those donations dedicated to child relief, to disaster aid, and to overseas development are overstated, while donations to religious purposes are substantially less frequent than in the original dataset.[19]

Concerns about selection bias due to matching the data can be dispelled when it comes to the subset of donors in the charity market set[20]: the representative household is barely smaller (-4.6812%), earns only slightly less income (-3.8028%) and is situated in a 1.5314% smaller locality. Gifts, by contrast, are significantly higher on average: the subset of organisations in

[19] The classification of organisations used here is that chosen by the GfK, so that the data in Table 4.4 refer to what participants of the survey declare. This does not necessarily correspond to the DZI-classification. I refer to these data anyway, because they reflect to what cause donors *believe* their gift to contibute to. Deviations are not substantial when it comes to the broad classification, as is demonstrated in Appendix B. Concerning the categorisation of types of relief organisations, though, the lack in discrimanotory power becomes evident. For instance, the majority of donors that claim to support development projects, give to organisations that classify themselves as *primarily* dedicated to religion, or health. On the other hand, health organisations are, apparently, mainly supported for reasons of disaster relief.

[20] Cf. Table 4.5.

Table 4.4: Distribution of Gifts by Organisation Type

Type of Organisation	Full set	Merged set
Relief	114,395	34,483
	(81.28)	(98.92)
Animal relief	7,588	52
	(5.39)	(0.15)
Environment	6,655	238
	(4.73)	(0.68)
Culture	5,889	11
	(4.18)	(0.03)
Other	6,218	76
	(4.42)	(0.22)
Total	140,745	34,860
	(100.00)	(100.00)

Type of Relief Organisation	Full set	Merged set
Religion	33,517	707
	(29.20)	(2.05)
Children	29,655	14,630
	(25.84)	(42.43)
Disaster	27,279	10,605
	(23.77)	(30.75)
Health	12,054	2,563
	(10.50)	(7.43)
Development	8,461	5,640
	(7.37)	(16.36)
Education	355	15
	(0.31)	(0.04)
Other	3,463	323
	(3.02)	(0.94)
Total	114,784	34,483
	(100.00)	(100.00)

Percentages in parentheses.

Classification following the GfK survey design.

Table 4.5: Merged Dataset: Summary Statistics

	mean	sd	median	p25, p75
Giftsize[1)]	30.3231	61.9430	20	10 , 30
Annual gift[2)]	96.08	193.92	40.00	15.00 , 100.00
Nr. of gifts[3)]	6.5687	13.2053	2	1 , 6
HH income[4)]	2459.32	1071.17	2375.00	1,625 , 3,125
Age[4)]	49.1922	15.67882	52	37 , 67
HH size[4)]	2.3620	1.114585	2	2 , 3
Children[4)]	0.2759	0.6521	0	0 , 0
City size[4)]	252,949	507,160	35,000	7,500 , 150,000
Ed. quartile[4)]	2.4792	1.1374	2	2 , 4
Alms dummy[1)]	0.0904	0.2867	0	0 , 0
Reg. / spons.[5)]	0.1769	0.3817	0	0 , 0
Gifts rev.[6)]	13,915,390	26,712,080	2,656,632	714,824 , 10,394,930
Total rev.[6)]	27,112,590	62,752,110	5,530,644	1,371,453 , 17,076,510
Frs. share[7)]	0.1391	0.0872	0.15	0.05, 0.15
Frs. exp.[8)]	3,621,393	9,440,639	690,803	120,267 , 2,606,505
F. exp. (adj.)[9)]	3,468,141	9,022,283	650,073	117,493 , 2,505,893
Return to f.[6)]	7.4785	6.0310	5.5554	3.2583 , 10.6327

1) Number of observations: *34,860* (gifts); 2004: *5,311* ; 2005: *9,243* ; 2006: *6,986* ; 2007: *6,479* ; 2008: *6,841*.

2) Number of obs.: *11,002* (household years); Consistent with 2.0731 per household.

3) Number of obs.: *5,307* (households); Last centile ranges from 66 to 202 gifts.

4) Number of obs.: *5,307* .

5) Number of obs.: *5,307* ; Regular donor, and / or sponsor.

6) Number of obs.: *498* (organisation years); 149 organisations.

7) Number of obs.: *498* ; Fundraising share computed from class means.

8) Number of obs.: *498* ; Fundraising expenditures approximated as described in Section 4.2.2 (frs. share · total rev.).

9) Number of obs.: *498* ; Fundraising expenditures as in 8), yet adjusted for disparities in expenditures and revenues, cf. Table 4.2.

the merged dataset receives 10.6392% higher particular donations than the representative DZI-organisation. It is noteworthy that for each of these variables, the standard deviation is smaller than in the respective original dataset, implying more homogenous gifts, or givers. This is not surprising since the restriction to DZI-organisations directs the focus to the institutionalised charity market. Gifts to the unsheltered on the street, support for relatives, neighbours and friends, or alms unrelated to the churchly relief organisations do not enter the merged dataset, which also explains why donations are higher, on the whole.

Regarding the nonprofit organisations that survive the matching process, selection bias is far more pronounced. The representative GfK-household tends to support overproportionately large charities (total revenues are by some 59% higher in the dataset than over all DZI-organisiations, gifts revenues even by 115%). The right-skewedness of both the total and gifts revenues' distributions becomes more pronounced. Most strikingly, the median of total revenues decreases, while the mean substantially rises. Besides, the measure of fundraising share (0.1391) is higher with respect to what I calculated from the original DZI-panel (0.1281), yet now comes quite close to the average share reported by the DZI itself (0.1419). Obviously, donors make overproportionate gifts to charities that rely less on them, due to major revenues from other sources.[21] This may be arrtibuted to the fact that such charities are better able to cross-finance elaborate fundraising campaigns without excessively increasing their fundraising share in *total* expenditures.

To summarise, the bias in the selected sample is predominantly due to a restriction in organisations, and not to an alarming donor selection. The matching process does not generally omit entire households, but that subset or their donations that is not directed to the well-established charity market. Besides, it is quite natural that large organisations are overstated in relation to the original sample. These organisations are large partly because they attract more gifts, and the dataset is constructed on a donation basis rather than on organisation-level. The following overview contrasts the charity market dataset's characteristics with those of its parent datasets:

- Donations: the fraction directed to relief organisations is considerably overstated, at 98.92% (81.28%); the amount given per single donation rises more than 10%, namely to 30.31 Euros (27.41);

[21] One should not mistake this effect for an overall measure of crowding-in through government grants, and / or program service. It is more likely to express the relevance of trustworthiness and competence, which many donors see as reflected in the sheer size of an organisation.

- Donors: selection bias is mainly innocuous (income, gender, education, household size, annual gift, . . .); the number of years a household donates in, is more unevenly distributed yet;
- Charities: selection bias towards large organisations with considerable revenues from sources other than donations, yet higher fundraising shares.

To prescind from selection bias, there are further characteristics worth mentioning. First, donor commitment is in fact not very pronounced, apart from donors that claim to make regular gifts to a particular cause (17.69%). While the total number of gifts averages around 6.6 (in five years), only 11,002 household years can be observed, that is, just over 2 years of appearance per household. There is reasonable concern that this uneven distribution of gifts over time hints at impulsive giving due to exogenous shocks, such as the 2004 Tsunami (and not to variations in fundraising effort). And in fact, 63.47% more donations are made in 2005, compared to the average over 2006 through 2008, and 18.27% more in 2004. The lack in constancy over time also points at the fact that, in response to extraordinary events, donors tend to rely on large, well-established organisations. The regressions in Section 4.3.2 address this problem with year dummies for 2004 and 2005.

Second, only one, yet large, organisation remains that reports zero fundraising, and only for one year (2007). 53 gifts were made to this organisation in that precise year. Third, the annual gift is very much in line with what the GfK reports, and similarly right-skewed as is household income. Fourth, around 9% of gifts are alms made during mass. These are certainly not all alms, but only those that are made to the churchly relief organisations in the DZI-dataset.

Adjusting the approximation of fundraising expenditures brings about lower overall levels of fundraising, while driving the distribution towards higher skewness (5.0565) and kurtosis (33.0789). These values come closer to those in the original DZI-dataset, where a large number of small fundraisers are dominated by few very large organisations.

My measure of return to fundraising (gift revenues related to fundraising expenditures) is consistent with the notion that charities renounce net revenue maximisation. On average, the marginal Euro dedicated to fundraising returns about 7.47 Euro worth of additional donations.[22]

[22] Note that the reported figures on return to fundraising (rtf) predicate on $1<rtf<21$, in order to exclude those organisation years that state no costs of fundraising at all. This restriction counts out the 53 donations mentioned above.

4.3 Analysis

The objective of this chapter is to investigate the ambiguous effect of fundraising on the intensive margin, i. e., to capture the impact of fundraising on the amount donated, using different measures of solicitation intensity. Section 4.3.1 addresses problems associated with characteristics of the charity market dataset. It describes basic manipulations necessary to ensure an efficient estimation, and to facilitate statistical inference. Section 4.3.2 outlines the estimation results, and discusses their implications.

4.3.1 Preliminary Manipulations

Ideally, an estimator is centered on the true value and, for statistical inference, with a known distribution. For analytical convenience, and for efficiency reasons, the estimator should be asymptotically normally distributed, with a small variance-covariance matrix of the estimator (VCE). Heteroskedasticity of the underlying data can critically harm the estimation quality, since the standard deviations of the error terms are not constant for any given value of the exogenous variable. The quality of the desired prediction hence depends on the level of the exogenous variable.

Table 4.6: Giftsize and Income Distributions

	giftsize[1)]	ln(giftsize)	income[1)]	ln(income)
mean	3,032.308	7.5042	249,771	12.4282
median	2,000	7.6009	237,500	12.3779
sd	6,194.303	0.9593	105,481	0.4686
skewness	26.3376	0.0974	0.4539	-0.7490
kurtosis	1,484.197	4.0418	2.3778	4.4311

1) Euro-Cents.

Besides, a normal probability distribution for the measured data cannot simply be assumed. As Table 4.6 indicates, the endogenous variable `giftsize` varies greatly across donations, with a standard deviation of more than twice the mean of 3,032 Euro-Cents. The skewness value of 26.33576 indicates considerable right-skewness (where a value of 0 would imply symmetrically distributed data). For normally distributed data, the kurtosis is 3 , here it takes on a value of nearly 1,500 , which suggests exceedingly heavier (or: longer) tails than those of a normal distribution.

Household income will prove the most influential exogenous variable, so Table 4.6 also includes summary statistics for that measure.[23] Skewness shows to be less pronounced than in the case of the amount donated, yet still noteable.

Such skewed, thick-tailed distributions suggest a model with multiplicative rather than additive errors. Taking the natural logarithm of `giftsize` essentially eliminates skewness and excess kurtosis, as can be taken from Table 4.6 as well as from Figure 4.1, which presents the corresponding kernel density plots.[24] For better graph readability, the distributions are truncated at 220 and ln(220) Euros, respectively, whilst the last gift centile ranges from 200 to the overall maximum of 5,000 Euros.

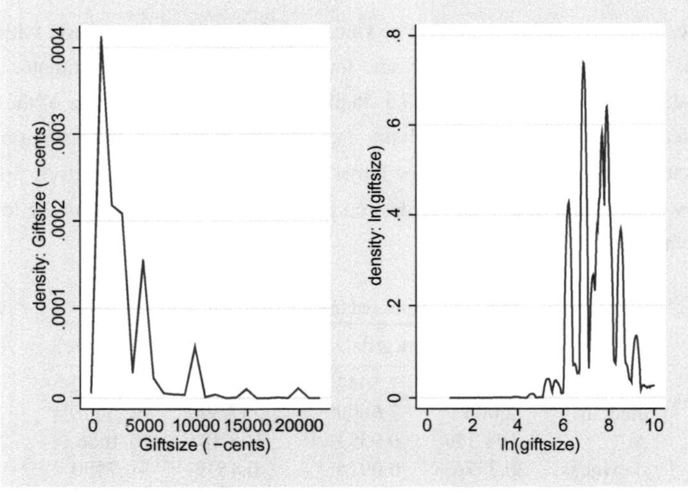

Figure 4.1: Kernel Density Estimates of Giftsize – Levels and Logs

If it were not for the truncation, the second graph in Figure 4.1, depicting the density of the natural logarithm of `giftsize`, would exhibit near symmetry just as proposed in Table 4.6. In both graphs, the evident lack of smoothness is due to the fact that households tend to donate "even" sums, which results in the marked peaks at 10, 20, 50, 100 Euros, and so on.

[23] Note that, since the endogenous variable is `giftsize`, the basis for the reported measures in Table 4.6 is the single donation, and not the donor. Summary statistics that are more informative about the characteristics of the households in the dataset, are presented in Table 4.5.

[24] Epanechnikov kernel, with bandwidths of 165 , and 0.09 , respectively.

Compared to donations, household-income is only slightly right-skewed; therefore taking the natural logarithm is not in order to change the distribution characteristics, but to ease interpretation: the resulting coefficients can be interpreted as elasticities. The same applies to fundraising expenditures, and other revenues, when used in the estimations in Section 4.3.2. Besides, a specification test via Box-Cox model[25] favours a loglinear model over a linear one. Though the corresponding Null Hypothesis is clearly rejected applying a Wald test, the maximum likelihood estimate of $\hat{\theta} = -0.0297$ is reasonably close to 0 and therewith suggests to apply the natural logarithm of `giftsize`.[26]

Another concern pertains to the time dimension. Individual giving is not constant over time, nor is the amount given, as stated in Table 4.7. One noticeable pattern is the increased giftsize in December, due to the widespread custom of practising charity on Christmas. Obviously, it affects the intensive margin, too, and not only the number of donations. The overproportianate December effect in 2004 can be largely attributed to the Southeast Asia Tsunami, just as can the relatively small one in 2005, where unusually high gifts were accordingly made at the *beginning* of the year.

This naturally raises the question, how these exogenous effects mingle with that of fundraising effort. Many charitable organisations concentrate their campaigns on the end of the year, so their impact is hard to separate from that due to the households' innate propensity to give on Christmas. Yet, by applying a December dummy, the coefficients of the fundraising variables capture the average of variations in fundraising *among* Decembers, and among non-Decembers. I address the Tsunami effect accordingly by including dummies for the years 2004 and 2005.

Before regression analysis, it is essential to examine which variables add to the explanation of giftsize variation while not violating parsimony requisitions. The merged dataset involves a number of variables, those of which are to be selected for analysis that prove influential for the focus of this chapter on donor-fundraiser relation. The first natural step is to check the pairwise

---

25 Cf., Box and Cox (1964).

26 The Box-Cox Transformation constitutes a generalisation of the estimation model that is supposed to render the residuals more closely normal and less heteroskedastic. But the transformation also embeds several common functional forms, and is therefore widely used as a method for testing functional forms. The reported $\hat{\theta} = -0.0297$ stems from the most general Box-Cox transformation. It allows for different parameters on the left-hand-side (dependent variable) and on the right-hand-side. Transformations of the independent variables were applied only to fundraising expenditures, other revenues, and `household income`. The rhs-parameter of $\hat{\lambda} = 0.7963$ actually favours a linear model over the logarithmic transformation.

Table 4.7: Extraordinary Giving Events

giftsize			
year	dec[1)]	mean	sd
2004	no	2,732.116	74.4408
2004	yes	4,167.998	155.187
2005	no	3,215.805	89.8661
2005	yes	3,902.907	243.2021
2006	no	2,605.200	44.2277
2006	yes	3,295.266	127.0163
2007	no	2,676.973	59.3335
2007	yes	3,699.072	241.1919
2008	no	2,670.568	75.5352
2008	yes	3,636.514	225.843

1) dec: December dummy.

correlations of the dependent variable and the potential regressor variables, so as to measure the strength and direction of the linear relationship between the two precise variables. Those pairs that exhibit a noticeable ($\rho > 0.05$) and significant ($p<0.05$) correlation, are highlighted in bold type in Table 4.8, with p-values given in parentheses.

The correlation measures in Table 4.8 are restricted to the numerical variables and dummies in the dataset, since correlations with categorical variables are not informative. The correlation with the ordinal variable `education quartile` should be interpreted with caution.

Significance is high in nearly all cases, which is not surprising given the size of the dataset, and given that the variables in the GfK-dataset are designed precisely to elucidate the effectivity of charities' fundraising activities. The variables `income` and education quartile are most markedly correlated with the endogenous variable `giftsize`. Fundraising expenditures exhibit a small, yet highly significant, negative correlation with the dependent variable.

Most of the exogenous variables are only weakly correlated among each other, with the exception of income that is quite distinctly linked to many of the others. The correlations with education and household size are quite plausible, that with gender empirically prevalent. The negative interdependency of income and fundraising expenditures may possibly be due to the fact that wealthy donors choose their supported cause following profounder considerations than simply responding to "the ask".

Table 4.8: Pairwise Correlations

Variables	Giftsize	Frs. exp.	Total rev.	Income	Gender	Age	Educ	Hh size	Children	Citysize
Giftsize	1.000									
Frs. exp.	-0.042	1.000								
	(0.000)									
Total rev.	-0.040	**0.855**	1.000							
	(0.000)	(0.000)								
Income	**0.148**	**-0.063**	-0.045	1.000						
	(0.000)	(0.000)	(0.000)							
Gender	0.026	-0.007	-0.010	**0.163**	1.000					
	(0.000)	(0.198)	(0.070)	(0.000)						
Age	-0.024	**0.060**	**0.051**	**-0.128**	**0.114**	1.000				
	(0.000)	(0.000)	(0.000)	(0.000)	(0.000)					
Educ	**0.083**	-0.033	-0.027	**0.288**	**0.197**	**-0.055**	1.000			
	(0.000)	(0.000)	(0.000)	(0.000)	(0.000)	(0.000)				
Hh size	0.004	-0.029	-0.012	**0.435**	0.026	**-0.394**	0.016	1.000		
	(0.402)	(0.000)	(0.022)	(0.000)	(0.000)	(0.000)	(0.004)			
Children	-0.004	-0.036	-0.027	**0.131**	**-0.065**	**-0.416**	0.030	**0.613**	1.000	
	(0.447)	(0.000)	(0.000)	(0.000)	(0.000)	(0.000)	(0.000)	(0.000)		
Citysize	0.018	0.034	0.030	-0.035	-0.031	0.035	0.031	**-0.163**	-0.082	1.000
	(0.001)	(0.000)	(0.000)	(0.000)	(0.000)	(0.000)	(0.000)	(0.000)	(0.000)	

The high, and obvious, correlation of `household size` and `number of children` leads to the elimination of the latter variable. It is reasonable to assume that the amount donated is – if it is – driven by the number of household members irrespective of whether additional members are children, or not.

Besides giving a first hint at potential causal relationships in the data, the correlation of independent variables among each other represents caveats on where to look for multicollinearity. Another consideration in this line is the application of variance inflation factors (VIFs), outlined in Table 4.9. The VIF of a variable measures whether its vector is orthogonal to each column of the design matrix for the regression on all other covariates. The square root of the VIF can be interpreted as a measure of how much larger the standard error is, compared with what it would be if that variable were completely uncorrelated with the other exogenous variables in the model.

For space reasons, I only report the fourth education quartile (the second and third have small positive effects, and their VIF is 1.45 and 1.67, respectively).

A fairly conservative rule of thumb is that a VIF>5 translates into high multicollinearity. Altogether, there is no substantial concern about multicollinearity, yet some valuable information can be gained from the factors, anyway. Fundraising expenditures' VIF of 1.47, for instance, means that the standard error for the coefficient is $\sqrt{1.47} = 1.2124$ times as large as, or: 21.24% larger than, it would be if fundraising expenditures were uncorrelated with all other predictor variables in the model. Since `other revenues` displays a relatively high, though still unworrying, VIF, and a very small and insignificant effect on giftsize in Model (1), this variable is eliminated from those regressions using absolute expenditures as a measure of fundraising effort. The highest VIFs apply to education, household size, income, and age, as expected due to their correlation among another. The overall maximum of 1.95 pertains to the alms dummy in specification (3), which is due to the fact that alms are attributed that fundraising intensity that applies to all activities involving a personal appeal.[27]

For specification analysis, a stepwise regression procedure is designed to identify the most parsimonious set of predictors that are yet most effective in predicting the dependent variable `giftsize`.

27 A further explanation of the variable fundraising intensity follows in Section 4.3.2.

Table 4.9: Specification Analysis: Variance Inflation

	(1) ln(giftsize)	(2) ln(giftsize)	(3) ln(giftsize)
lnadjfexp	-0.0244**		
	1.47		
fundshare		-0.4320**	
		1.17	
1.fundint			0.1260***
			1.45
2.fundint			0.0706
			1.47
3.fundint			-0.0980**
			1.89
4.fundint			0.2790***
			1.07
lnhhincm	0.5360***	0.535***	0.5400***
	1.43	1.43	1.43
lnrevoth	-0.0083	-0.0189***	-0.0159**
	1.49	1.08	1.05
gender	-0.0729	-0.0721	-0.0713
	1.09	1.09	1.09
age	-0.0010	-0.0010	0.0001
	1.40	1.41	1.46
ln(citysize)	0.0074	0.0067	0.0069
	1.06	1.06	1.06
hhsize	-0.1220***	-0.1220***	-0.1240***
	1.56	1.56	1.56
4.quarted	0.1750***	0.1740***	0.1780***
	1.83	1.84	1.84
1.sponsor	0.3420***	0.3240***	0.2750***
	1.25	1.21	1.28
1.timing	0.3260***	0.3250***	0.3210***
	1.04	1.04	1.06
alms dummy	-0.1340*	-0.1550**	-0.2180**
	1.06	1.16	1.95
year2004	0.0804***	0.0807***	0.0687**
	1.12	1.12	1.13
year2005	0.1210***	0.1180***	0.1050***
	1.09	1.09	1.10
dec dummy	0.2150***	0.2120***	0.2130***
	1.07	1.08	1.08
cons	1.2610*	1.1320*	0.9290

Observations: 34,860. VIF in second line.

* $p < 0.05$, ** $p < 0.01$, *** $p < 0.001$

The results of the specification analysis are illustrated in the following overview, while a discussion of variable definitions and implications for the actual estimation procedure is postponed to Section 4.3.2.

- Independent variables that prove most influential: `income`, `household size`, education quartile, `sponsor`, `timing`, December dummy, fundint and its interactions with fundraising expenditures;
- Independent variables that prove less influential: `gender`, ln(citysize), and `age` (only variable to increase BIC[28]), alms dummy, 2004 and 2005 year dummies, inducement and its interaction with fundraising expenditures ;
- Best set of predictors (according to BIC) excludes age, and replaces inducement (and interactions with fundraising expenditures) with fundraising intensity (and interactions with fundraising expenditures).

To address another concern, outliers often prove problematic when they shape up as influential observations. The dataset is quite homogenous, though, and most of the extreme values are elimininated due to the merging process, since these were often very small donations, e. g., to individuals on the street. There are 46 gifts larger than 500 Euros, 14 of which are again larger than 1,000 Euros. The treatment of a singular donation of 5,000 Euros, and of five extremely small donations is described in more detail in Appendix B.

Before presenting my regression results in the following section, there is one more characteristic of the dataset that analysis has to take into account. Panel-specific analysis enables a more detailed summary, and a more efficient estimation than standard OLS, and estimation with cluster-specific fixed effects. Yet, as already described in Section 4.2.1, panel estimation methods are not applicable for reasons of information loss, and prediction problems concerning missing entries. The second-best method to make concession to the data is to employ the donation-based dataset as it is, and to cluster on households. This does not conceal the within-variation (and therewith implicitly presuppose constant giving behaviour), but less degrees of freedom for the robust variance estimator mean higher hurdles for the significance of coeffi-

[28] Bayesian Information Criterion, emphasises parsimony more than the other common measures as adjR^2, and AIC, each of which embraces every additional variable in the specification.

cients. Besides, cross-sectional variation is likely to be more influential for identification than time series variation.[29]

As a standard, the analysis in Section 4.3.2 resorts to cross-section estimators with cluster-robust standard errors. If the only complication is that the error is correlated within clusters, then valid inference can be drawn. The results of plausible comparative regressions without, and with, correction for clusters imply that standard errors remain small, and therewith t-statistics maintain a sufficient size in all specifications used.

4.3.2 Estimation Results

This section begins by presenting regression results employing three different measures of fundraising. Then it will investigate how giving motivation influences the effect of fundraising effort on giftsize.

I employ three measures of fundraising effort, two of which are derived from the nonprofit dataset. Fundraising effort as it is valued by the organisation does not necessarily correspond to the effort as it is sensed by the individual donor. So, I employ a third measure that stems from the household survey, and therewith reflects as how intensive fundraising is *perceived* by the survey respondent in question.

- Absolute annual fundraising expenditures, (DZI) ; approximation employing the variable `fundraising share*total annual revenues`;
- `fundraising share` in total expenditures, (DZI) ; class means applied;
- Fundraising intensity, (GfK) ; reported `fundraising` measures assigned to five classes of fundraising intensity.

While fundraising expenditures and fundraising share are numerical variables, the third measure is constructed from qualitative statements the donor makes about the fundraising measure she encountered prior to the gift. The GfK offers a set of 64 preselected responses, and leaves room for hand-written entries, otherwise. The variable fundraising intensity, as derived from the reported fundraising measures, is specified as follows:

[29] Cf., e. g., Straub (1999).

- No fundraising, or missing entry (value: none/other, 0);
- Incidental, undirected fundraising: bulk mail, mass e-mail, advertisement (tv, www, radio / cinema), placard (value: incidental, 1);
- Independent information: friends, collegues, article / editorial (newspaper, internet), tv coverage (value: independent, 2);
- Personal appeal: direct solicitation, addressed envelope, alms, telephone, information booth (value: personal, 3);
- Personal involvement: cause directly related to donor, community of interest, warm glow (value: involved, 4).

The largest fraction of donations in the dataset is claimed to be made following a personal, or personalised, solicitation. A strikingly low number of donations results from more broadly targeted measures, which thwarts their usually much broader reach. Only very few donations relate to reasons of personal involvement, which alleviates the problem of how to evaluate these entries in terms of fundraising intensity.

Table 4.10: Fundraising Intensity

Item	Number	Percent
0.none/other	7,080	20
1.incidental	4,435	13
2.independent	6,399	18
3.personal	16,564	48
4.involved	382	1
Total	34,860	100

Table 4.11 reports estimation results for the three measures of fundraising, while setting aside the control variables.[30]

[30] Note that all estimations employ the same controls, with a single exception: the logarithm of `other revenues` is omitted from Estimation (1) because of its strong correlation with `total revenues`, which again forms part of the respective fundraising measure. This was also pointed out earlier in this chapter. Control variables are: ln(other rev.), gender, ln (citysize), hh size, education quartile (index), sponsorship dummy, timing (index), alms dummy, 2004 dummy, 2005 dummy, december dummy.

The coefficients are plausible for all variables of interest, and for the control variables (not reported in the table). Besides, the coefficients of the control variables education quartile (only the fourth quartile is significant), `household size`, `timing`, `sponsor`, and the December dummy are stable to changes in the fundraising measure throughout. They imply that the most highly educated give around 17% more, that every additional household member results in around 12% lower gifts, that gifts in the context of a sponsorship are around 34% higher, spontaneous gifts around 32% lower, and that donations in December are around 21% higher.

Considering the results reported in Table 4.11, my findings are consistent with a negative effect of fundraising on the intensive margin. While the prevalent determinant of the donation is disposable household income, fundraising effort still accounts for some variation in gift-size. Estimation (1) offers a measure of fundraising elasticity that suggests that a percentage increase in fundraising expenditures calls for an average reduction of the donation by 0.03 percent. This is a considerably small, yet statistically significant effect.

Table 4.11: Fundraising Measures

	(1) ln(giftsize)	(2) ln(giftsize)	(3) ln(giftsize)
ln(hh income)	0.5361***	0.5353***	0.5404***
	(0.0468)	(0.0467)	(0.0472)
ln(adj. frs. exp.)	-0.0315***		
	(0.0075)		
Frs. share (%)		-0.432**	
		(0.144)	
1.Frs. intensity			0.126***
			(0.0375)
2.Frs. intensity			0.0706
			(0.0478)
3.Frs. intensity			-0.0980**
			(0.0355)
Observations	34,860	34,860	34,860
R^2	0.1442	0.1444	0.1505
$adjR^2$	0.1438	0.1441	0.1500

Controls omitted from output. Standard errors in parentheses.

* $p < 0.05$, ** $p < 0.01$, *** $p < 0.001$

The coefficient of fundraising share should be interpreted as a semi-elasticity, since the parameter measures the proportionate change in $E(y|\mathbf{x})$ as x_j varies, rather than the level change. The proposition is then that of a percentage change in response to a one-unit variation in fundraising share. Since the latter is given in percent, though, the coefficient of 0.4 again suggests a fundraising *elasticity*. The measure in Estimation (2) is substantially larger and reflects the fact that fundraising share standardises the fundraising effort over the whole scale of charities, while absolute fundraising expenditures are predominantly driven by organisation size. So, for the measure in Estimation (1), the positive correlation between organisation size and donation size which was discussed in Section 4.2.3 largely countervails the negative impact of fundraising effort.

The measure of fundraising intensity in Estimation (3) displays a plausible pattern, and equally suggests an overall negative impact on the intensive margin. Low levels of fundraising intensity result in 12.6 percent higher gifts than no fundraising at all. Yet, a further increase countervails, and eventually overcompensates this effect, resulting in roughly ten percent lower gifts than in the case of no fundraising. This finding corresponds to earlier observations that contributions and fundraising effort exhibit an inversely u-shaped relation.[31]

When operating a solicitation campaign, the fundraiser faces a trade-off between adding revenue from new contributors, and losing revenue from other donors due to their aversion to fundraising expenditures. Because of these countervailing effects, aggregate contributions will be a nonlinear function of fundraising expenditures. Since a strictly positive return on the extensive margin can be taken for granted, the finding of an overall negative effect on the intensive margin is not surprising. Rather, an overall optimal fundraising effort is most likely to displace part of the gifts by, e. g., the repeatedly solicited.

The impact of donor motivation is undisputed in non-profit market research as well as in the economic literature, in general. An online survey of 4,000 individuals carried out by Hope Consulting, for instance, results in the allocation of donors to six "behavioral segments"[32]: Repayer (23% of respondents, 17% of donations), Casual Giver (18%, 18%), High Impact (16%, 12%), Faith-Based (16%, 18%), See the Difference (14%, 10%), and Personal Ties (13%, 25%). The classification is self-explanatory except for the distinction between impact-

---

[31] See, e. g., Straub (1999), Manzoor and Straub (2005). Similar implications are also proposed in Chapter 3, and by von Kotzebue and Wigger (2008) from a theoretical point of view.

[32] Hope Consulting (2010), p. 22.

oriented and difference-seeking donors. The former directs gifts to causes with high social returns, the latter to local or small recipients.

The GfK Charity Scope proposes a comparable measure of donor motivation. The categorical variable inducement to give captures information on why the respondent chooses to support the particular cause, and takes on the following values:

- Other, or missing entry (value: other, 0);
- Cause-orientation (value: purpose, 1);
- Trustworthy organisation (value: trustworthy, 2);
- Regular gift (value: habitual, 3);
- Transparent gift assignment (value: account, 4);
- Regional ties (value: regional, 5).

It remains unclear how "trustworthy" organisations (2) intermingle with those that give a transparent account (4) on the proceedings of the gift allocation. Many survey respondents are likely to condition their trust in an organisation on its transparent (financial) conduct. Conceptually, the classification is not as convincing as Hope Consulting's, and there are only few parallels when it comes to donor segregation, for instance regional ties. Even if they seemingly describe opposite giving behaviour, casual giving on the one hand, and regular giving on the other, also stem from the same attitude of not thoroughly scrutinising every single gift. My dataset emphasises attitudes towards the *charitable organisation*, whereas the "behavioral segments" build on attitudes towards the charitable cause. In that light, the GfK-classification even is better suited for an analysis of fundraising impact, although it appears somewhat arbitrary in terms of segmentation.

It has to be noted that this variable groups donors as to which attitudes drive their giving choices primarily on the *extensive* margin. However, it is instructive to analyse the consequences of these convictions on the intensive margin, too. The by far largest fraction of donations can be assigned to donors that give to support the cause advocated by the respective charitable organisation. Apart from that, trustworthiness and transparency prove most decisive for donor attraction.

Table 4.12: Inducement to Give

Item	Number	Percent
0.other	2,556	7
1.purpose	21,331	61
2.trustworthy	5,267	15
3.habitual	2,910	8
4.account	2,796	8
5.regional	0	0
Total	34,860	100

Table 4.13 reports estimation results that reflect the impact of donors' attitudes towards the charity, and of the intensity of the fundraising measure employed, while restricting presentation to statistically significant coefficients. Again, the set of control variables applies to both estimations equally.

The giving pattern suggested by Estimation (1) can be summarised as follows. Not surprisingly, the size of the donation is highly sensitive to convictions about the supported cause, and about transparency. Purpose-related donations are nearly double as high as the baseline gift. Since both of the significantly reactive donor groups are interested in the destination of the gift, they can be assigned to the same basic motivation: they give primarily for altruistic reasons. However, trustworthiness displays no significant effect on giving, which may be due to the inaccuracy of donor segmentation discussed above, or may indicate that it is decisive only on the extensive margin.

The fundraising impact displays a more differentiated pattern, too, when taking donors' attitudes toward charities into account. The overall fundraising measure implies a small positive – yet statistically insignificant – impact, which is however overcompensated by the fundraising aversion of those donors that give for reasons based on altruistic considerations.

Estimation (2) reports the results of another set of interactions employed to receive a more differentiated picture of fundraising impact. While fundraising expenditures capture how extensively a charity employs solicitation measures, fundraising intensity measures how perceptible they are to the donors. In a way of speaking, fundraising intensity might approximate the quality of fundraising campaigns, whereas the other measures of fundraising effort describe how *extensively* the particular measures are being conducted.

Table 4.13: Interactions

	(1) ln(giftsize)	(2) ln(giftsize)
ln(hh income)	0.538***	0.536***
	(0.0468)	(0.0467)
ln(adj. frs. exp.)	0.0211	-0.0119
	(0.0148)	(0.0112)
1.Inducement 1)	0.966***	
	(0.285)	
4.Inducement 1)	0.744*	
	(0.333)	
1.induce x ln(adjfexp)	-0.0637***	
	(0.0175)	
4.induce x ln(adjfexp)	-0.0474*	
	(0.0208)	
1.Fundraising intensity 2)		-0.592*
		(0.243)
3.Fundraising intensity 2)		0.423
		(0.239)
4.Fundraising intensity 2)		1.421*
		(0.631)
1.fundint x ln(adjfexp)		0.0449**
		(0.0151)
3.fundint x ln(adjfexp)		-0.0320*
		(0.0146)
4.fundint x ln(adjfexp)		-0.0707
		(0.0390)
Observations	34,860	34,860
$adjR^2$	0.1462	0.1525

Controls omitted from output. Standard errors in parentheses.
* $p < 0.05$, ** $p < 0.01$, *** $p < 0.001$.
1) Inducement to give: 1=`purpose`, 4=`account`.
2) Fundraising intensity: 1=`incidental`, 3=`personal`, 4=`involved`.
1) and 2) Other values: no significant impact.

Again, the coefficient of fundraising expenditures indicates no genuine significant effect, when examined in a more differentiated context. However, regarding those donors that give in response to less intensive measures, more extensive fundraising alleviates the basically lower individual gift. The pattern goes into reverse when more intensive measures are considered: Gifts are initially higher than the baseline, but extensive fundraising tends to be punished by donors.

Especially in the case of a personal appeal (p-value of 0.077), or involvement, gifts are higher in response to the relatively high intensity indeed, but thereamong gifts directed to organisations that use fundraising measures more extensively decrease by a marginal 3%, or even 7% (p-value of 0.070), again.[33] An implication of this pattern could be that organisations should make use of personalised fundraising measures, but not excessively. They should, for instance, not immoderately invest in the outward quality of direct mailings.

4.4 Concluding Remarks

This chapter contributes to the literature on charitable giving by exploiting combined data from two sources, one of which is representative of the German population, the other of which reflects a substantial fraction of charitable organisations operating in Germany. A convincing link of donor- and organisation-level datasets is very rare in the literature. A suchlike dataset that comprises more than one single charity market segment does, to my knowledge, not exist to date.

The merging process shows to basically sustain the characteristics of donors, yet selects only that fraction of their donations that is conferred to well-established charities. The study can therefore be said to investigate the fundraising effect on the size of voluntary donations, restricting attention to well-established nonprofit organisations in Germany.

The analysis makes use of three different measures of fundraising effort in order to assess its impact on donations. Yet, the coefficients can solely elucidate the fundraising effect on the intensive margin, since the dataset is based on donations that are actually carried out. Absolute fundraising expenditures, and the fundraising share in total expenditures are derived from the organisation-level dataset, whereas the measure of fundraising intensity stems from

[33] In the table, only p-values under 0.05 are labelled. Still, the two quoted cases exhibit a reasonably high statistical significance.

the household-level dataset, and therewith elucidates as how intensive households perceive the fundraising measures that lead to their gift.

The estimations deliver intuitive results, while the sheer size of the dataset allows to detect rather small effects, too. The implications can be summarised as follows:

- Fundraising coefficients are negative throughout, and stable to different specifications;
- Increasing fundraising intensity initially results in higher gifts, yet subsequently countervails, and eventually overcompensates this effect;
- The amount donated is highly sensitive to altruistic convictions;
- Less intensive measures: more extensive fundraising enhances initially lower individual giving;
- More intensive measures: more extensive fundraising decreases the initially higher individual donation;
- Secondary findings, robust to various specifications:
  - The most efficient model specification of donor-fundraiser-relation incorporates fundraising intensity;
  - Disposable household income accounts for the largest impact on the variation in giftsize; given the precise month of the gift, the respective elasticity is over 53% in all specifications;
  - Sponsorship contracts entail around 34% higher gifts;
  - Spontaneous gifts are around 32% lower;
  - Donations in December are around 21% higher;
  - Donors in the top education quartile make around 17.5% higher gifts than all others;
  - An additional household member results in around 12% lower gifts;
  - On average, the marginal Euro dedicated to fundraising returns about 7.47 Euro worth of additional donations;

- The results of an investigation of the effect of tax exemptions on giving is relegated to Appendix B, for lack of robustness and discriminatory power.

The widely acknowledged positive impact of fundraising on the extensive margin, combined with the negative one on the intensive margin that is suggested by this study, may indicate a reversed u-shaped relation between fundraising effort and donation. The negative effect of fundraising is remarkably low, depending on which measure is employed. Yet, this is not surprising: the fundraising elasticity of donations can be expected to be quite low, since gifts are often driven by habit, or by a sense of acquittal, and not in all cases by a thorough investigation of charitable causes (and the corresponding fundraising scheme).

Finally, the analysis of this fairly large – and to my knowledge, unique – dataset confirms what is often implied by donor-level surveys: demographic characteristics of a donor are important to predict her giving behaviour, but more so are her convictions. Impact orientation, as reflected by sponsorship contracts, or altruistic considerations, significantly influence the amount a donor is ready to sacrifice, and by far more than bare fundraising effort.

5 Summary

This study is concerned with the charity market in Germany. An outline of the economic literature on collective goods and voluntary donations is followed by a theoretical model of strategic fundraising, and by an empirical investigation of donor-fundraiser interaction.

The theoretical part presents philanthropy as a strategic conflict between recipient and contributor, where excessive fundraising can be limited by anticipatory bounteousness, or by regulatory means, i- e., tax exemption of charitable gifts. While not offering a fully-fledged positive model of fundraising, this approach elucidates the problem of inefficiency associated with the common fundraising process. Moreover, it states a case in favour of granting tax benefits to contributors that goes beyond the standard Pigouvian argumentation.

The empirical part introduces a new dataset that builds on extensive surveys of the donor as well as the organisation side of the charity market in Germany. The link between donor and recipient is direct, as opposed to earlier studies in that field. The merged dataset is used to investigate the donation-fundraising relation on the intensive margin. The fundraising impact is small but significant, and shows to be sensitive to donor convictions as well as to the donor's perception of fundraising intensity.

There is potential for much deeper investigation of the donor-fundraiser-government interrelation, yet better data on the organisation-level would be desirable. The DZI collects much exacter financial data than it publishes in the Spenden-Almanach, yet was not willing to disclose them for use in this project. The data would enable the application of instruments for fundraising[1], especially when it comes to an estimation of the effect of tax exemptions on fundraising, which again would allow to shed some light on the corresponding implications in the theoretical model presented in Chapter 3.

---

1 Andreoni and Payne (2011) propose a set of variables that measure the financial solidity of organisations, i. e., total liabilities and total occupancy expenses, because fundraising effort is assumed to react to variations in these figures, while an individual's propensity to give is not directly affected.

Bibliography

[1] Abrams, B. A. and M. A. Schmitz (1978): *The Crowding Out Effect of Governmental Transfers on Private Charitable Contributions*, Public Choice 33, pp. 29-39.

[2] Abrams, B. A. and M. A. Schmitz (1984): *The Crowding Out Effect of Governmental Transfers on Private Charitable Contributions: Cross Sectional Evidence*, National Tax Journal 37, pp. 563-568.

[3] Admati, A. R. and M. Perry (1991): *Joint Projects without Commitment*, Review of Economic Studies 58, pp. 259-276.

[4] Andreoni, J. (1988): *Privately Provided Public Goods in a Large Economy: the Limits of Altruism*, Journal of Public Economics 35, pp. 57-73.

[5] Andreoni, J. (1989): *Giving with Impure Altruism: Applications to Charity and Ricardian Equivalence*, Journal of Political Economy 97, pp. 1447-1458.

[6] Andreoni, J. (1990): *Impure Altruism and Donations to Public Goods: a Theory of Warm-Glow Giving*, The Economic Journal 100, pp. 464-477.

[7] Andreoni, J. (1998): *Toward a Theory of Charitable Fundraising*, Journal of Political Economy 106, pp. 1186-1213.

[8] Andreoni, J. (2006): *Leadership Giving in Charitable Fundraising*, Journal of Public Economic Theory 8, pp. 1-22.

[9] Andreoni, J. (2006a), *Philanthropy*, in: Kolm, J. C. and G. Mercier-Ythier (eds.), HANDBOOK OF THE ECONOMICS OF GIVING, ALTRUISM, AND RECIPROCITY, VOL. 2: APPLICATIONS, North-Holland, pp. 1201-1269.

[10] Andreoni, J. and T. Bergstrom (1996): *Do Government Subsidies Increase the Private Supply of Public Goods?*, Public Choice 88, pp. 295-308.

[11] Andreoni, J. and A. A. Payne (2003): *Do Government Grants to Private Charities Crowd Out Giving or Fund-raising?*, American Economic Review 93, pp. 792-812.

[12] Andreoni, J. and A. A. Payne (2011): *Is crowding out due entirely to fundraising? Evidence from a panel of charities*, Journal of Public Economics 95, pp. 334–343.

[13] Auten, G. E., C. T. Clotfelter and H. Sieg (2002): *Charitable Giving, Income, and Taxes: An Analysis of Panel Data*, American Economic Review 92, pp. 371-382.

[14] Bac, M. and P. K. Bag (2003): *Strategic Information Revelation in Fundraising*, Journal of Public Economics 87, pp. 659-679.

[15] Bag, P. K. and S. Roy (2008), *Repeated Charitable Contributions under Incomplete Information*, The Economic Journal 118, pp. 60-91.

[16] Bagnoli, M. and B. L. Lipman (1989): *Provision of Public Goods: Fully Implementing the Core through Private Contributions*, Review of Economic Studies 56, pp. 583-601.

[17] Becker, G. S. (1974): *A Theory of Social Interactions*, Journal of Political Economy 82, pp. 1063-1093.

[18] Bénabou, R. and J. Tirole (2006): *Incentives and Prosocial Behavior*, American Economic Review 96, pp. 1652-1678.

[19] Bergstrom, T., L. Blume and H. Varian (1986): *On the Private Provision of Public Goods*, Journal of Public Economics 29, pp. 25-49.

[20] Bernheim, B. D. (1986): *On the Voluntary and Involuntary Provision of Public Goods*, American Economic Review 76, pp. 789-793.

[21] Bilodeau, M. and N. Gravel (2004): *Voluntary Provision of a Public Good and Individual Morality*, Journal of Public Economics 88, pp. 645-666.

[22] Bilodeau, M. and A. Slivinski (1997): *Rival Charities*, Journal of Public Economics 66, pp. 449-467.

[23] Blackwell, C. and M. McKee (2003): *Only for My Own Neighborhood? Preferences and Voluntary Provision of Local and Global Public Goods*, Journal of Economic Behavior and Organization 52, pp. 115-131.

[24] Bliss, C. and B. Nalebuff (1984): *Dragon-Slaying and Ballroom Dancing: The Private Supply of a Public Good*, Journal of Public Economics 25, pp. 1-12.

[25] Blumkin, T. and E. Sadka (2007): *A Case for Taxing Charitable Donations*, Journal of Public Economics 91, pp. 1555-1564.

[26] Bolton, G. and A. Ockenfels (2000): *ERC - A Theory of Equity, Reciprocity and Competition*, American Economic Review 90, pp. 166-193.

[27] Borgloh, S. (2008): *What Drives Giving in Extensive Welfare States? The Case of Germany*, ZEW Discussion Paper No. 08-123, Mannheim: ZEW.

[28] Borgonovi, F. (2006): *Do Public Grants to American Theatres Crowd-out Private Donations?*, Public Choice 126, pp. 429-451.

[29] Bowles, S. and H. Gintis (2005): *Can Self-interest Explain Cooperation?*, Evolutionary and Institutional Economics Review 2, pp. 21-41.

[30] Box, G. E. P. and D. R. Cox (1964): *An Analysis of Transformations*, Journal of the Royal Statistical Society, Series B, Vol. 26, pp. 211-243.

[31] Brekke, K. A., S. Kverndokk and K. Nyborg (2003): *An Economic Model of Moral Motivation*, Journal of Public Economics 87, pp. 1967-1983.

[32] Chan, K. S., R. Godby, S. Mestelman and R. A. Muller (1997): *Equity Theory and the Voluntary Provision of Public Goods*, Journal of Economic Behavior and Organization 32, pp. 349-364.

[33] Charness, G. and M. Rabin (2002): *Social Preferences: Some Simple Tests and a New Model*, Quarterly Journal of Economics 117, pp. 817-869.

[34] Clarke, E. (1971): *Multipart Pricing of Public Goods*; Public Choice 8, pp. 19-33.

[35] Clotfelter, C. T. (1985): FEDERAL TAX POLICY AND CHARITABLE GIVING; University of Chicago Press.

[36] Cornes, R. and T. Sandler (1984): *Easy Riders, Joint Production, and Public Goods*, The Economic Journal 94, pp. 580-598.

[37] Diamond, P. (2006): *Optimal Tax Treatment of Private Contributions for Public Goods with and without Warm Glow Preferences*, Journal of Public Economics 90, pp. 897-919.

[38] Duncan, B. (1999): *Modeling Charitable Contributions of Time and Money*, Journal of Public Economics 72, pp. 213-242.

[39] Duncan, B. (2002): *Pumpkin Pies and Public Goods: the Raffle Fundraising Strategy*, Public Choice 111, pp. 49-71.

[40] Duncan, B. (2004): *A Theory of Impact Philanthropy*, Journal of Public Economics 88, pp. 2159-2180.

[41] DZI (2010): DZI SPENDEN-ALMANACH 2010/11, Berlin: Deutsches Zentralinstitut für soziale Fragen.

[42] Eckel, C. C., P. J. Grossman and R. M. Johnston (2005): *An Experimental Test of the Crowding Out Hypothesis*, Journal of Public Economics 89, pp. 1543-1560.

[43] Falk, A. and U. Fischbacher (2006): *A Theory of Reciprocity*, Games and Economic Behavior, 54, pp. 293-315.

[44] Fehr, E. and U. Fischbacher (2002): *Why do Social Preferences Matter - The Impact of Non-Selfish Motives on Competition, Cooperation and Incentives*, The Economic Journal 112, pp. C1-C33.

[45] Fehr, E. and S. Gächter (2002): *Fairness and Retaliation: The Economics of Reciprocity*, Journal of Economic Perspectives 14, pp. 159-181.

[46] Fehr, E. and K. Schmidt (1999): *A Theory of Fairness, Competition, and Cooperation*, Quarterly Journal of Economics 114, pp. 817-868.

[47] Fehr, E. and K. Schmidt (2003): *Theories of Fairness and Reciprocity - Evidence and Economic Applications*, in: Dewatripont, M., L. P. Hansen and S. J. Turnovsky (eds.): ADVANCES IN ECONOMICS AND ECONOMETRICS - 8TH WORLD CONGRESS, ECONOMETRIC SOCIETY MONOGRAPHS; Cambridge University Press.

[48] Field, A. J. (2001): ALTRUISTICALLY INCLINED? THE BEHAVIORAL SCIENCES, EVOLUTIONARY THEORY, AND THE ORIGINS OF RECIPROCITY; University of Michigan Press.

[49] Fong, C. (2001): *Social Preferences, Self-interest, and the Demand for Redistribution*, Journal of Public Economics 82, pp. 225-246.

[50] Frey, B. S., and S. Meier (2004): *Social Comparisons and Pro-social Behavior: Testing "Conditional Cooperation" in a Field Experiment*, American Economic Review 94, pp. 1717-1722.

[51] Gintis, H., S. Bowles, R. Boyd and E. Fehr (2005): MORAL SENTIMENTS AND MATERIAL INTERESTS: THE FOUNDATIONS OF COOPERATION IN ECONOMIC LIFE; MIT Press.

[52] Glazer, A. and K. A. Konrad (1996): *A Signaling Explanation for Charity*, American Economic Review 86, pp. 1019-1028.

[53] Groves, T. (1973): *Incentives in Teams*, Econometrica 41, pp. 617-631.

[54] Gruber, J. (2004): *Pay or Pray? The Impact of Charitable Subsidies on Religious Attendance*, Journal of Public Economics 88, pp. 2635-2655.

[55] Gruber, J. and D. M. Hungerman (2007): *Faith-based Charity and Crowd-out During the Great Depression*, Journal of Public Economics 91, pp. 1043-1069.

[56] Guttman, J. M. (1978): *Understanding Collective Action: Matching Behavior*, American Economic Review 68, pp. 251-255.

[57] Hammerstein, P. (ed.) (2003): GENETIC AND CULTURAL EVOLUTION OF COOPERATION; MIT Press.

[58] Harbaugh, W. T. (1998a): *What Do Donations Buy? A Model of Philanthropy Based on Prestige and Warm Glow*, Journal of Public Economics 67, pp. 269-284.

[59] Harbaugh, W. T. (1998b): *The Prestige Motive for Making Charitable Transfers*, American Economic Review 88, pp. 277–282.

[60] Henrich, J. (2004): *Cultural Group Selection, Coevolutionary Processes and Large-Scale Cooperation*, Journal of Economic Behavior and Organization 53, pp. 3-35.

[61] Henrich, J., R. Boyd, S. Bowles, C. Camerer, E. Fehr, H. Gintis and R. McElreath (2001): *In Search of Homo Economicus: Behavioral Experiments in 15 Small-Scale Societies*, American Economic Review 91, pp. 73-78.

[62] Henrich, J., R. Boyd, S. Bowles, C. Camerer, E. Fehr and H. Gintis (2004): FOUNDATIONS OF HUMAN SOCIALITY: ECONOMIC EXPERIMENTS AND ETHNOGRAPHIC EVIDENCE FROM FIFTEEN SMALL-SCALE SOCIETIES; Oxford University Press.

[63] Hillier, B. (1997): THE ECONOMICS OF ASYMMETRIC INFORMATION; St. Martin's Press.

[64] Hochman, H. M. and J. D. Rogers (1973): *Utility Interdependence and Income Transfers through Charity*, in: Boulding, K. E. (ed.): TRANSFERS IN AN URBANIZED ECONOMY; Belmont.

[65] Holländer, H. (1990): *A Social Exchange Approach to Voluntary Cooperation*; American Economic Review 80, pp. 1157-1167.

[66] Hope Consulting, LLC (2010): Money for Good. The US Market for Impact Investments and Charitable Gifts from Individual Donors and Investors, http://hopeconsulting.us/money-for-good/ (last accessed: December 15, 2012).

[67] Isaac, R., J. Walker and A. Williams (1994): *Group Size and the Voluntary Provision of Public Goods - Experimental Evidence Utilizing Large Groups*, Journal of Public Economics 54, pp. 1-36.

[68] Kant, I. (1785): GRUNDLEGUNG ZUR METAPHYSIK DER SITTEN; Johann Friedrich Hartknoch.

[69] Kant, I. (1907): FUNDAMENTAL PRINCIPLES OF THE METAPHYSICS OF ETHICS; 3rd edition, Longmans. English translation by T. K. Abott.

[70] Kaplow, L. (1995): *A Note on Subsidizing Gifts*; Journal of Public Economics 58, pp. 469-477.

[71] Karlan, D. and J. A. List (2007): *Does Price Matter in Charitable Giving? Evidence from a Large-Scale Natural Field Experiment*, American Economic Review 97, pp. 1774-1793.

[72] Khanna, J., J. Posnett and T. Sandler (1995): *Charity Donations in the UK: New Evidence based on Panel Data*, Journal of Public Economics 56, pp. 257-272.

[73] Kingma, B. R. (1989): *An Accurate Measure of the Crowd-out Effect, Income Effect, and Price Effect for Charitable Contributions*, Journal of Political Economy 97, pp. 1197-1207.

[74] Kirchsteiger, G. and C. Puppe (1997): *On the Possibility of Efficient Private Provision of Public Goods through Government Subsidies*, Journal of Public Economics 66, pp. 489-504.

[75] Konrad, K. A. (1998): *Local Public Goods and Central Charities*, Regional Science and Urban Economics 28, pp. 345-362.

[76] Laffont, J. J. (1975): *Macroeconomic Constraints, Economic Efficiency, and Ethics: an Introduction to Kantian Economics*, Economica 42, pp. 430-437.

[77] Ledyard, J. (1995): *Public Goods: a Survey of Economic Research*, in: Kagel, J. and A. E. Roth (ed.): THE HANDBOOK OF EXPERIMENTAL ECONOMICS; Princeton University Press.

[78] List, J. A. and D. Lucking-Reiley (2002): *The Effects of Seed Money and Refunds on Charitable Giving: Experimental Evidence from a University Capital Campaign*, Journal of Political Economy 110, pp. 215-233.

[79] Mandeville, B. (1724): THE FABLE OF THE BEES: OR, PRIVATE VICES, PUBLICK BENEFITS; 3rd edition, J. Tonson.

[80] Manzoor, S. H. and J. D. Straub (2005): *The robustness of Kingma's crowd-out estimate: evidence from new data on contributions to public radio*, Public Choice 123, pp. 463–476.

[81] Margolis, H. (1982): SELFISHNESS, ALTRUISM AND RATIONALITY; Cambridge University Press.

[82] Marx, L. M. and S. A. Matthews (2000): *Dynamic Voluntary Contribution to a Public Project*, Review of Economic Studies 67, pp. 327-358.

[83] Meier, S. (2006): THE ECONOMICS OF NON-SELFISH BEHAVIOUR; Edward Elgar.

[84] Mellström, C. and M. Johannesson (2005): *Crowding Out in Blood Donation: Was Titmuss Right?*, Göteborg University Working Papers in Economics 180.

[85] Morgan, J. (2000): *Financing Public Goods by Means of Lotteries*, Review of Economic Studies, 67, pp. 761-784.

[86] Morgan, J. and M. Sefton (2000): *Funding Public Goods with Lotteries: An Experiment*, Review of Economic Studies, 67, pp. 785-810.

[87] Olson, M. (1965): THE LOGIC OF COLLECTIVE ACTION; Harvard University Press.

[88] Payne, A. A. (1998): *Does the Government Crowd-out Private Donations? New Evidence from a Sample of Non-profit Firms*, Journal of Public Economics 69, pp. 323-345.

[89] Peloza, J. and P. Steel (2005): *The Price Elasticities of Charitable Contributions: A Meta-Analysis*, Journal of Public Policy and Marketing, 24, pp. 260-272.

[90] Posnett, J. and T. Sandler (1989): *Demand for Charity in Private Non-Profit Markets*, Journal of Public Economics 40, pp. 187-200.

[91] Rabin, M. (1993): *Incorporating Fairness into Game Theory and Economics*; American Economic Review 83, pp. 1281-1302.

[92] Randolph, W. C. (1995): *Dynamic Income, Progressive Taxes, and the Timing of Charitable Contributions*, Journal of Political Economy 103, pp. 709-738.

[93] Ribar, D. C. and M. O. Wilhelm (2002): *Altruistic and Joy-of-Giving Motivations in Charitable Behavior*, Journal of Political Economy 110, pp. 425-457.

[94] Roberts, R. D. (1984): *A Positive Model of Private Charity and Public Transfers*, Journal of Political Economy 92, pp. 136-148.

[95] Roberts, R. D. (1987): *Financing Public Goods*, Journal of Political Economy 95, pp. 420-437.

[96] Romano, R. and H. Yildirim (2001): *Why Charities Announce Donations: a Positive Perspective*, Journal of Public Economics 81, pp. 423-447.

[97] Rose-Ackerman, S. (1982): *Charitable Giving and "Excessive" Fundraising*, Quarterly Journal of Economics 97, pp. 193-212.

[98] Roth, A. E., V. Prasnikar, M. Okuno-Fujiwara and S. Zamir (1991): *Bargaining and Market Behavior in Jerusalem, Ljubljana, Pittsburgh, and Tokyo: An Experimental Study*, American Economic Review 81, pp. 1068-1095.

[99] Samuelson, P. A. (1954): *The Pure Theory of Public Expenditure*, Review of Economics and Statistics 36, pp. 387-389.

[100] Shang, J. and R. T. A. Croson (2009): *A Field Experiment in Charitable Contribution: The Impact of Social Information on the Voluntary Provision of Public Goods*, The Economic Journal 119, pp. 1422-1439.

[101] Steinberg, R. (1987): *Voluntary Donations and Public Expenditures in a Federalist System*, American Economic Review 77, pp. 24-36.

[102] Steinberg, R. (1991): *Does Government Spending Crowd out Donations? Interpreting the Evidence*, Annals of Public and Cooperative Economics 62, pp. 591-617.

[103] Straub, J. D. (2004): *Fundraising and Crowd-out of Charitable Donations: New Evidence from Contributions to Public Radio*, Working Paper, Department of Economics, Texas A&M University.

[104] Sugden, R. (1984): *Reciprocity: the Supply of Public Goods through Voluntary Contributions*, The Economic Journal 94, pp. 772-787.

[105] Titmuss, R. M. (1970): THE GIFT RELATIONSHIP; Allen and Unwin.

[106] Varian, H. R. (1994): *Sequential Contributions to Public Goods*, Journal of Public Economics 53, pp. 165-186.

[107] Vesterlund, L. (2003): *The Informational Value of Sequential Fundraising*, Journal of Public Economics 87, pp. 627-657.

[108] Vickrey, W. (1961): *Counterspeculation, Auctions, and Competitive Sealed Tenders*, Journal of Finance 16, pp. 8-37.

[109] von Kotzebue, A. and B. U. Wigger (2008): *Charitable Giving and Fundraising: When Beneficiaries Bother Benefactors*, Discussion Paper 2008-03, Tax Institute Nuremberg.

[110] von Kotzebue, A. and B. U. Wigger (2010): *Private Contributions to Collective Concerns: Modelling Donor Behaviour*, Cambridge Journal of Economics 34, pp. 367-387.

[111] von Kotzebue, A. and B. U. Wigger (2013): *An Empirical Investigation of Donor-Fundraiser Interaction*, Working Paper, Economics Department, Karlsruhe Institut für Technologie (KIT).

[112] Warr, P. G. (1982): *Pareto Optimal Redistribution and Private Charity*, Journal of Public Economics 19, pp. 131-138.

[113] Warr, P. G. (1983): *The Private Provision of a Public Good is Independent of the Distribution of Income*, Economics Letters 13, pp. 207-211.

[114] Wilke, B. (2010): *Zur Situation des deutschen Spendenwesens im Jahr 2010*, in: Deutsches Zentralinstitut für soziale Fragen (ed.), DZI SPENDEN-ALMANACH, pp. 6-9.

[115] Wolfelsperger, A. (1999): *Sur l'existence d'une solution kantienne du problème des biens collectifs*, Revue Economique 50, pp. 879-902.

[116] Young, D. J. (1989): *A "Fair Share" Model of Public Good Provision*, Journal of Economic Behavior and Organization 11, pp. 137-147.

A Appendix: Theory

Proof of Proposition 1

A Pareto-efficient allocation solves the programme

$$\max_{\{m \geq d \geq 0, f \geq 0\}} \quad B = u(m-d) + v(d-f, f),$$

subject to a predefined net payoff $\overline{b} = d - f$ for the beneficiary. The set of Pareto-efficient (d, f)-bundles is implicitly defined by

$$d = \overline{b} + f, \tag{A.1}$$

$$-u'(m - \overline{b} - f) + v_2(\overline{b}, f) \leq 0, \quad \text{with} = 0, \text{ if } f > 0. \tag{A.2}$$

Choose $\overline{b} = d^* - f^*$, and add on equations (3.3) and (3.4) to see that (d^*, f^*) solves equations (A.1) and (A.2). Thus, (d^*, f^*) is Pareto-efficient. Now assume, contradictory to what is stated in Proposition 1, that $(d_e, f_e) \neq (d^*, f^*)$ also is efficient. Then, (d_e, f_e) must be consistent with $-u' + v_1 = 0$ from (3.5) and $d_e > 0$, as well as with $-u' + v_2 = 0$ from (A.2) and $f_e > 0$. This implies that (d_e, f_e) is consistent with $-v_1 + v_2 = 0$. From (3.3) and (3.4) and the concavity of u and v, it follows that $(d_e, f_e) = (d^*, f^*)$. This is a contradiction. ■

Proof of Proposition 2

Graphically, the proposition follows from the tangency of the indifference curves I_b and I_B in $(\hat{d}, \hat{f})$. Formally, $(\hat{d}, \hat{f})$ is the solution to

$$\max_{\{m \geq d \geq 0, f \geq 0\}} \quad B = u(m-d) + v(d-f, f),$$

subject to $d - f = d_e - f_e$. Obviously, for a given bundle (d_e, f_e), this results in a Pareto-efficient allocation. ■

Proof of Proposition 3

It is to demonstrate that by additional fundraising, the best bundle accessible to the beneficiary remains (d_e, f_e), the equilibrium outcome of the natural fundraising game.

The beneficiary can obviously enforce this allocation even when the benefactor makes the first draw. After all, the latter cannot cease to react to fundraising activities, since the resulting loss in the beneficiary's net resources would still marginally harm her own utility, also when f exceeds $\hat{f}$. However, the payoff the beneficiary would gain with (d_e, f_e) is precisely the one she receives from the allocation $(\hat{d}, \hat{f})$. And applying the concept of epsilon altruism as in Section 3.2, she will refrain from further fundraising.

Starting from $(\hat{d}, \hat{f})$, the beneficiary thus spends additional effort f on fundraising. The benefactor will react by solving

$$\max_{d \geq 0} \quad u\big[m - (\hat{d} + d)\big] + v\big[(\hat{d} + d) - (\hat{f} + f), (\hat{f} + f)\big].$$

The first-order condition reads

$$-u'\big[m - (\hat{d} + d)\big] + v_1\big[(\hat{d} + d) - (\hat{f} + f), (\hat{f} + f)\big] = 0. \tag{A.3}$$

This establishes total giving $\hat{d} + d$ as a function of total fundraising $\hat{f} + f$, i. e.,

$$\hat{d} + d = g(\hat{f} + f),$$

so that (A.3) may be restated as

$$-u'\big[m - g(\hat{f} + f)\big] + v_1\big[g(\hat{f} + f) - (\hat{f} + f), (\hat{f} + f)\big] = 0. \tag{A.4}$$

I will now show that a unique interior solution $\hat{f} + f$ exists that solves equation (A.4). Differentiating the left hand side of (A.4) with respect to f yields

$$u''g' + v_{11}(g' - 1) + v_{12}.$$

The beneficiary chooses f so that $g' = 1$. Consequently, the expression simplifies to

$$u''g' + v_{12}.$$

By the implicit function theorem it follows that

$$g' = \frac{v_{11} - v_{12}}{u'' + v_{11}},$$

and hence

$$u''g' + v_{12} = \frac{u''v_{11} - v_{11}v_{12}}{u'' + v_{11}} < 0.$$

Thus, $\hat{f} + f = f_e$ and $\hat{d} + d = g(\hat{f} + f) = g(f_e) = d_e$. ■

Example 1

Let $v = \frac{1}{\gamma} b^{\gamma} f^{\gamma} - \frac{\alpha}{\gamma} f^{\gamma}$. Then the derivative with respect to f is given by

$$v_2 = b^{\gamma} f^{\gamma-1} - \alpha f^{\gamma-1}.$$

Since $b = d - f \leq m$, it follows that fundraising is annoying, $v_2 < 0$, as long as $\alpha > m^{\gamma}$. The benefactor's most-favoured allocation (d^*, f^*) now solves

$$-(m - d^*)^{\gamma-1} + (d^* - f^*)^{\gamma-1} f^{*\gamma} \lesseqgtr 0, \quad \text{with} = 0, \text{ if } m > d^* > 0,$$
$$-(d^* - f^*)^{\gamma-1} f^{*\gamma} + (d^* - f^*)^{\gamma} f^{*\gamma-1} - \alpha f^{\gamma-1} \leq 0, \quad \text{with} = 0, \text{ if } f^* > 0.$$

Since $\alpha > m^{\gamma} \geq d - f$, it follows that

$$-(d^* - f)^{\gamma-1} f^{\gamma} + (d^* - f)^{\gamma} f^{\gamma-1} - \alpha f^{\gamma-1} < 0$$

for $f > 0$, so that $f^* = 0$. This, in turn, implies

$$-(m - d)^{\gamma-1} + (d - f^*)^{\gamma-1} f^{*\gamma} = (m - d)^{\gamma-1} < 0$$

for $d > 0$, so that $d^* = 0$. Thus the benefactor's most-favoured allocation reads

$$(d^*, f^*) = (0, 0).$$

The equilibrium allocation in the natural setting, (d_e, f_e), is exactly the one that also applies when $\alpha = 0$ (see equation (A.5) in the Appendix, Example 2), i. e.,

$$(d_e, f_e) = \left(m + 1 - \sqrt{m+1}, \sqrt{m+1} - 1\right),$$

if $\gamma = \frac{1}{2}$.

In the benefactor's most-favoured feasible allocation, $(\hat{d}, \hat{f})$, the fundraising level is given by $\hat{f} = 0$. Thus, the benefactor must guarantee the beneficiary a net benefit amounting to $d = d_e - f_e$. For $\gamma = \frac{1}{2}$, this is

$$d_e - f_e = m - 2(\sqrt{m+1} - 1),$$

so that the benefactor's most-favoured feasible allocation reads

$$(\hat{d}, \hat{f}) = \left(0, m - 2(\sqrt{m+1} - 1)\right).$$

Example 2

For $u = \frac{1}{\gamma} c^\gamma$ and $v = \frac{1}{\gamma} b^\gamma f^\gamma$, the benefactor's most-favoured allocation (d^*, f^*) solves

$$-(m - d^*)^{\gamma-1} + (d^* - f^*)^{\gamma-1} f^{*\gamma} \lesseqgtr 0, \quad \text{with} = 0, \text{ if } m > d^* > 0,$$
$$-(d^* - f^*)^{\gamma-1} f^{*\gamma} + (d^* - f^*)^\gamma f^{*\gamma-1} \leq 0, \quad \text{with} = 0, \text{ if } f^* > 0.$$

It can be readily verified that

$$(d^*, f^*) = \left(m - 1, \frac{1}{2}(m - 1)\right),$$

if $\gamma = \frac{1}{2}$, and that

$$(d^*, f^*) = (0, 0),$$

if $\gamma = 1$.

Now consider an equilibrium allocation with a given subsidy rate $\sigma \in [0,1]$. The first-order condition determining the benefactor's donation reads

$$-(1-\sigma)(m-d)^{\gamma-1}+(d-f)^{\gamma-1}f^{\gamma} \lesseqgtr 0, \quad \text{with} = 0, \text{ if } m > d > 0.$$

For $\gamma = \frac{1}{2}$, this implies the reaction function

$$d(f) = \frac{[m+(1-\sigma)^2]f}{(1-\sigma)^2+f},$$

and for $\gamma = 1$,

$$d(f) = \begin{cases} 0, & \text{if } f < 1-\sigma, \\ m, & \text{if } f \geq 1-\sigma. \end{cases}$$

The fundraising level chosen by the beneficiary in anticipation of the benefactor's response is then determined by

$$f = (1-\sigma)\sqrt{m+(1-\sigma)^2} - (1-\sigma)^2,$$

if $\gamma = \frac{1}{2}$, and by

$$f = 1-\sigma,$$

if $\gamma = 1$. Let $\sigma = 0$. Then it can be inferred that the equilibrium EQL is given by

$$(d_e, f_e) = \left(m+1-\sqrt{m+1}, \sqrt{m+1}-1\right), \tag{A.5}$$

if $\gamma = \frac{1}{2}$, and by

$$(d_e, f_e) = (m, 1),$$

if $\gamma = 1$. In a subsidy equilibrium $\sigma > 0$ holds true, so that

$$(d_\sigma, f_\sigma) = \Big(m+(1-\sigma)^2 - (1-\sigma)\sqrt{m+(1-\sigma)^2},$$
$$(1-\sigma)\sqrt{m+(1-\sigma)^2} - (1-\sigma)^2\Big),$$

if $\gamma = \frac{1}{2}$, and

$$(d_\sigma, f_\sigma) = (m, 1 - \sigma),$$

if $\gamma = 1$.

A Pareto-efficient subsidy equilibrium with an interior subsidy rate solves equation (3.16) in Section 3.5, which is given by

$$-(m - d_\sigma)^{\gamma-1} + (d_\sigma - f_\sigma)^\gamma f_\sigma^{\gamma-1} = 0$$

in the present example. For $\gamma = \frac{1}{2}$ this is equivalent to

$$f - (d_\sigma - f_\sigma)(m - d_\sigma) = 0,$$

which gives

$$\sigma^* = \frac{1}{2}(3 - m).$$

For $\gamma = 1$, eq. (3.16) now becomes

$$-(m - d_\sigma) + d_\sigma - f_\sigma = 0,$$

which implies

$$\sigma^* = 2 - m.$$

Note that in case of $\gamma = 1$ there are infinitely many efficient subsidy equilibria with an interior subsidy rate. To see this, consider the payoffs of the beneficiary and the benefactor in a subsidy equilibrium,

$$b_\sigma = m - 1 + \sigma,$$
$$B_\sigma = (m - 1 + \sigma)(1 - \sigma).$$

Since b_σ strictly increases in σ, every subsidy equilibrium that is consistent with a rate of $\sigma \in [\frac{1}{2}(2-m), 1]$ is Pareto-efficient. The subsidy rate $\sigma = \frac{1}{2}(2-m)$ that maximises B_σ corresponds to SUB_1 in Table 1.

Proof of Proposition 5

In the $(\hat{d},\hat{f})$ allocation the beneficiary's payoff is given by $\hat{d}-\hat{f}$, i. e., the beneficiary's payoff is the same as obtained in a subsidy equilibrium with $\sigma = 0$. According to equation (3.14), the beneficiary's payoff in the subsidy equilibrium is increasing in σ. Since a Pareto-efficient subsidy equilibrium requires $\sigma > 0$ by Propositions 1 and 2, it follows that the beneficiary strictly prefers the allocation $(d_{\sigma^*}, f_{\sigma^*})$. Since both the allocation $(d_{\sigma^*}, f_{\sigma^*})$ and the allocation $(\hat{d},\hat{f})$ are Pareto-efficient, the benefactor strictly prefers $(\hat{d},\hat{f})$. ■

Example 3

The benefactor's most-favoured feasible allocation $(\hat{d},\hat{f})$ must guarantee the beneficiary a net endowment amounting to $d-f = d_e - f_e$. For $\gamma = \frac{1}{2}$, this is

$$d_e - f_e = m - 2(\sqrt{m+1} - 1).$$

Thus, the benefactor's most-favoured feasible allocation solves

$$\max_{\{m \geq d \geq 0, f \geq 0\}} \quad 2\,(m-d)^{1/2} + 2\,(d-f)^{1/2} f^{1/2},$$

subject to

$$d - f = m - 2(\sqrt{m+1} - 1).$$

It can be readily verified that the solution reads

$$(\hat{d},\hat{f}) = \left(\frac{(m+1)\,[m-2(\sqrt{m+1}-1)]}{m+1-2(\sqrt{m+1}-1)}, \frac{2(\sqrt{m+1}-1)\,[m-2(\sqrt{m+1}-1)]}{m+1-2(\sqrt{m+1}-1)} \right).$$

B Appendix: Empirics

Correspondence of Organisation Types (GfK vs. DZI)

Differences in how organisations describe themselves, and how their mission is perceived by their donors (in a particular giving event), are captured in the following table, contrasting the variables `type of addressee` (GfK), and `type of organisation` (DZI). Entries deviating from the main diagonal indicate conflicting classifications.

Table B.1: Types of Charities: GfK-respondents vs. DZI-classification

Type of addressee (GfK)	Type of organisation (DZI) other	relief	culture	animalrel	environm	Total
other	0	76	0	0	0	76
relief	1	34,482	0	0	0	34,483
culture	0	5	6	0	0	11
animalrel	0	0	0	51	1	52
environm	0	0	0	0	238	238
Total	1	34,563	6	51	239	34,860

Table B.2 examines the subclassification of relief organisations, and to that end contrasts the variables `type of relief org.` (GfK), and `type of relief org.` (DZI). Here, marked deviations from the main diagonal imply a poor accordance of the classifications, as proposed by the organisations on the one hand, and recognised by donors, on the other. In case of a natural disaster, donors obviously support organisations with the intention to provide disaster relief. These organisations will actually function to that end in case of a disaster, but may otherwise – or, generally – consider themselves as dedicated to health, to child relief, or to development issues.

Table B.2: Types of Relief Org.: GfK-respondents vs. DZI-classification

Type of rel. org. (GfK)	Type of relief org. (DZI) other	child	relig	health	develop	disas	educ	Total
other	247	1	3	50	17	0	4	322
children	34	10,026	120	2,667	38	0	1,745	14,630
religion	0	7	276	168	30	0	226	707
health	47	5	0	2,511	0	0	0	2,563
development	0	0	2,315	2,083	1,235	0	7	5,640
disaster	14	8	1	9,241	31	1,290	20	10,605
education	0	0	0	0	31	0	15	15
Total	342	10,047	2,715	16,720	1,351	1,290	2,017	34,482

Merging process

1. Assign four-digit code to each `addressee` (as listed in the DZI-publications, for example: "Bischöfliches Hilfswerk Misereor e.V.": "BMIS");

2. Identify short sequence that a) defines (unique, if possible) common property of all probable transcriptions/ paraphrases/ abbreviations used by respondents, and b) is as immune as possible to misspellings (ex.: "mise" excludes, e. g., "Missionswerk", and is moreover not easily misspelled), and perform search;

3. Display list of results (ex.: Apart from entries choosing the appropriate number from the preselection list, the 709 observations include several hand-written entries: "Misereor" 44, "Misereor eV": 11, "Misereor e.V.": 13, "Bischöfliches Hilfswerk Misereor": 6, "Bischöfl. HW Misereor": 3, "Miseror": 4, "Miseror e.V": 1, . . .);

4. Replace results of search by four-digit code (ex.: "BMIS"); begin replace-routine with most exclusive result (ex. "Bischöfliches Hilfswerk Misereor"), end with most inclusive (ex. "Misereor"); starting with "Misereor" will lead to entries such as "Bischöfl. HW BMIS", obliterating the value of "mise" in identifying the desired entries in a potentially necessary subsequent search step;

5. If necessary, and for purpose of control, identify additional (possibly more inclusive) sequence, and repeat routine (ex. "Kollekte MIS." detected by means of "mis");

6. Corresponding transformations are also effected for the categorical variables `fundraising`, and `inducement to give`, which also consist of predominantly hand-written entries.

Outliers

Six outliers detected, five of which pertain to extremely small gifts of ten Euro-Cents and less. These observations are deleted from the dataset.

One outlier is due to the extreme donation of 5,000 Euros by household 9194 (whilst reporting a net monthly income of 1,250). The distribution of its 179 gifts is displayed in Table B.3, and it suggests a typo (given the household's age, income, and especially its gift distribution). Due to somewhat expectable confusion (the GfK questionnaire requires to fill in Euro, these are subsequently transformed into Euro-Cents), the data state "50000" where the household likely filled in "5" (The routine of multiplying with 100 was likely applied twice). A total of 115 entries with this amount represent 64% of all the household's gifts, followed by 27% with 1,000 Euro-Cents; only two gifts, or 1.12% are higher than 2,000 Euro-Cents, and they are directed at other adressees than the 500,000 Euro-Cent gift). The value is altered from 500,000 to 500.

Table B.3: Household 9194: Gift Distribution

Gift (Euro-Cents)	Freq.	Percent	Cum.
500	115	64.25	64.25
1,000	48	26.82	91.06
1,500	8	4.47	95.53
1,841	2	1.12	96.65
2,000	3	1.68	98.32
5,000	1	0.56	98.88
6,000	1	0.56	99.44
500,000	1	0.56	100.00
Total	179	100.00	

Tax Exemptions

The crowding effect of government grants is well explored. An ex-ante intention of the empirical analysis was to scrutinise the effect of a tax privilege of donations on giving and fundraising, either by exploiting a relevant amendment (in effect since January 2007) by means of a regression discontinuity approach, or by exploiting the corresponding within-household variation. The former approach delivered no result, and what is more, it could not be determined whether that is because there simply is no effect, or because the data are not suited (for reasons of a too small number of cases, and of donors' potential lack of information about the amendment). The latter analysis is presented in the following passages, together with its prohibitive limitations.

Table B.4: Tax Price of Giving

	(1) ln(giftsize)	(2) ln(giftsize)	(3) ln(giftsize)
ln(houshold income)	0.539***	0.500***	0.536***
	(0.047)	(0.056)	(0.047)
Tax price		-0.258	
		(0.159)	
Alms dummy			-0.134*
			(0.055)
ln(fundraising exp.)	-0.020*	-0.023**	-0.024**
	(0.009)	(0.008)	(0.008)
ln(other revenues)	-0.010	-0.009	-0.009
	(0.006)	(0.006)	(0.006)
Observations	34860	34860	34860
$adjR^2$	0.143	0.143	0.144

Controls omitted from output. Standard errors in parentheses.
* $p < 0.05$, ** $p < 0.01$, *** $p < 0.001$

The dataset at hand offers two possible alleys to potentially grasp the effect of tax exemptions on giftsize:

- Estimate the tax price of giving, depending on the individual marginal tax rate (the mtr was rather roughly approximated resorting to net income, the number of children, and the year-related German tax scheme);
- Exploit variations using the alms dummy (since alms are most commonly conveyed without requesting a contribution receipt).

The analysis delivers the following results:

- Coefficients on tax price and on alms dummy are negative, as expected;
- Caveat: imperfect collinearity of tax price and income (induced by linear-progressive tax scheme), makes the use of instruments inevitable;
- Using the alms dummy might permit interpretation of variation in tax price for a given household (711 of 5,307 households report alms *and* ordinary donations);
- Negative coefficients in Table B.4 might suggest a positive effect of tax exemptions on giftsize;
- Caveat: lower gifts during mass are more likely due to other reasons, e. g., to a crowding effect of the church tax in Germany, or to the habit of regularly contributing small amounts rather than making one large donation.

In conclusion:

- The effect of a tax privilege of donations is not convincingly seizable with the dataset at hand;
- Better organisation-level data would permit the use of instruments, and a more exact approximation of fundraising expenditures.

MIX
Papier aus verantwortungsvollen Quellen
Paper from responsible sources
FSC® C105338

If you have any concerns about our products,
you can contact us on
ProductSafety@springernature.com

In case Publisher is established outside the EU,
the EU authorized representative is:
Springer Nature Customer Service Center GmbH
Europaplatz 3, 69115 Heidelberg, Germany

Printed by Libri Plureos GmbH
in Hamburg, Germany